Lucid Dreaming

A Step-By-Step Beginners Guide to Controlling Your Dreams

Layla Moon

Table of Contents

Table of Contents

4 FREE Gifts

To help you along your spiritual journey, I've created 4 FREE bonus eBooks.

You can get instant access by signing up to my email newsletter below.

On top of the 4 free books, you will also receive weekly tips along with free book giveaways, discounts, and so much more.

All of these bonuses are 100% free with no strings attached. You don't need to provide any personal information except your email address.

To get your bonus, go to:

https://dreamlifepress.com/four-free-gifts

Or scan the QR code below

Spirit Guides for Beginners: How to Hear the Universe's Call and Communicate with Your Spirit Guide and Guardian Angels

Guided by Moon herself, inspired by her own experiences and knowledge that has been passed down by hundreds of generations for thousands of years, you'll discover everything you need to know to;

- Understanding what the call of the universe is
- How to hear and comprehend it
- Knowing who and what your spirit guides and guardian angels are
- Learning how to connect, start a conversation, and listen to your guides
- How to manifest your dreams with the help of the cosmic source
- Learning how to start living the life you want to live
- And so much more...

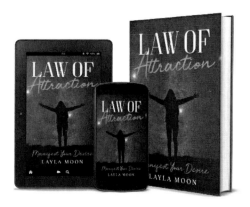

Law of Attraction: Manifest Your Desire

Learn how to tap into the infinite power of the universe and manifest everything you want in life.

Includes:

- Law of Attraction: Manifest Your Desire ebook
- Law of Attraction Workbook
- Cheat sheets and checklists so make sure you're on the right path

Hoodoo Book of Spells for Beginners: Easy and effective Rootwork, Conjuring, and Protection Spells for Healing and Prosperity

Harness the power of one of the greatest magics. Hoodoo is a powerful force ideal for holding negativity at bay, promoting positivity in all areas in your life, offering protection to the things you love, and ultimately taking control of your destiny.

Inside, you will discover:
- How to get started with Hoodoo in your day-to-day life
- How to use conjuration spells to manifest the life you want to live
- How casting protection spells can help you withstand the toughest of times
- Break cycles of bad luck and promote good fortune throughout your life
- Hoodoo to encourage prosperity and financial stability
- How to heal using Hoodoo magic, both short-term and long-term traumas and troubles
- Remove curses and banish pain, suffering, and negativity from your life
- And so much more…

Book of Shadows

A printable PDF to support you in your spiritual transformation.

Within the pages, you will find:

- Potion and tinctures tracking sheet
- Essential oils log pages
- Herbs log pages
- Magical rituals and spiritual body goals checklist
- Tarot reading spread sheets
- Weekly moon and planetary cycle tracker
- And so much more

Get all the resources for FREE by visiting the link below

https://dreamlifepress.com/four-free-gifts

Introduction

Freedom is taking control of your own life.

–Willie Nelson

I wasn't brought up in a compassionate or gentle home. For most of my youth, I was surrounded by angry people and uncomfortable situations. Though I loved my family and cherished every minute with them, things weren't easy. I bounced in and out of poverty, became lost in the brutal streets of New York, and often lost who I was as an individual.

For a long time, I felt like a character stuck in someone else's nightmare. I didn't know who I was or what I was meant to do. I had no control. I was a phantom of a little African American girl in a very big world.

I longed for something greater than what I had been granted. I wanted a normal life with dreams of ponies, princesses, and ballet dancers. I wanted to go to school and get good grades. I wanted someone to love and cherish me - my own Cinderella story.

Instead, I was frequently plagued by nightmares - and paranoia, depression, and anxiety followed me wherever I went.

I waded through toxic relationships, poverty, and heartache, waiting for the nightmare to end.

One day, I let a friend coax me into joining her on a meditation retreat on the outskirts of Brooklyn. I skeptically agreed, only because I would get a comfortable bed to sleep in and food for the night at a cheaper price than I could get anywhere else.

Wow! was my life changed.

It wasn't that I didn't believe in the benefits of meditation. I had been indulging in various meditation practices for years without much reward. The art seemed rather lax, and the effects were never as profound as I expected. Still, I trudged along with false enthusiasm.

In the last session, we were taught how to practice lucid dreaming. As I fell into the familiar darkness of slumber, I started noticing signs that I was dreaming. The walls waved at me from across the room; but walls can't wave. Pictures of the

Great Buddha began to drip paint onto the tiled floor; but pictures don't drip. My body began to turn to ice, even though it was a warm summer evening.

My mind noticed the onset of a nightmare. It had never done that before.

I pushed the walls back, sending them hurtling out across a sunny, sandy beach. The ice on my arms quickly melted as the warm summer breeze blasted past me, hugging my skin comfortingly. The melting pictures transformed into enormous scoops of vanilla ice cream held up by giant candy cones and drizzled in chocolate syrup. I had finally discovered one thing in my life that I could control. For the first time, I was the master of my mind.

After gaining the ability to control my dreams, I quickly learned how to control my life, my success, and my future. Over the next seven years, I went on to manifest the life I always dreamed of - the life I have today - and help others do the same.

Maybe you think the practice of lucid dreaming is just an indulgence in tomfoolery. I can guarantee you that this is not the case.

Using scientific evidence, this book will pull you into the paradigm of lucid dreaming and help you uncover even the most hidden parts of yourself.

This is THE comprehensive guide for lucid dreaming, not only providing a great in-depth explanation of what lucid dreaming is, but it will also take you by the hand in its step-by-step process to mastering the practice. Gaining control of your dreams has never been so easy.

With a collection of experiences described by writer Stephen King, scientist Albert Einstein, engineer Nicola Tesla, and actor Leonardo Di Caprio, this book is impossible to put away and will leave even the greatest skeptics curious.

This is not a spiritual awakening; it's not a religious practice. It is a life-changing tool.

Use it and find the power that lies within you.

PART 1

Everything You Need to Know About Lucid Dreaming

The science behind why people need sleep is fascinating - mostly because there is still so much that remains a mystery. For the most part, scientists believe that you need to sleep to rejuvenate and heal your mind after a busy day. It's also been stated that, without regular rest, your immune, psychological, and physical health becomes disrupted.

Sleep is a necessary part of your survival, but what about dreaming? What purpose does dreaming about a fanciful man in a purple hat and red trench coat serve in your everyday life? Why do some people see this stranger in their dreams while others don't? Why do some dream in color while others dream in black-and-white? And, why do so few people remember their dreams?

Hundreds of years ago, Shamans used lucid dreaming to heal people, prevent floods, appease the gods, and find guidance.

Today, lucid dreaming is practiced by people all over the world. Lucid dreaming helps athletes memorize field layouts and play scenarios. Artists and graphic designers use it to decipher how a space would look with different colors and objects. Even sound technicians are known to practice lucid dreaming to resolve cable clutter and spacing issues. For teachers, parents, and students, lucid dreaming is a time-savvy problem solver. Have you ever heard the notion *I'll sleep on it?* When you realize that you are dreaming while you're doing it, you can play out difficult-to-comprehend information in multiple ways until you understand it.

A lucid dream is an unforgettable experience. Its very nature is enchanting and mysterious. No one can explain why it exists. But it does, and what it can do for you is incredible.

Do you want to live in a bigger home? Do you wish for a job where you are appreciated? Do you wish to have a skill that can change the world? Do you dream of being the kind of teacher who has an enormous impact on the lives of children? Lucid dreaming can help you achieve your deepest desires.

Physically, lucid dreaming improves motor coordination, general awareness, and depth perception. It also alleviates stress and helps maintain general health.

Psychologically, it improves moods, creativity, planning, problem-solving abilities, and general empathy.

In the long term, it helps uncover your deepest fears and desires, alleviates trauma and stress, and aids in the development of ideas, thoughts, solutions, and understandings. It can help pave the way to your success.

I'm not saying that lucid dreaming will make you a millionaire or that you'll unearth God's next great plan. Heck, I'm not even saying that you'll be able to make your rent on time this month.

But, if you practice lucid dreaming regularly, your life will change, and you will be better for it.

Let me show you how.

CHAPTER 1

What Happens When You Dream?

The Brain and Sleeping

What does your brain look like while you're sleeping? If you could open your skullcap and peer into your cranium without passing out in fearful disgust, what would you see? Luckily, the electroencephalogram (EEG) was created for that exact purpose. Neuroscientists around the globe have used this fun little machine to uncover a variety of information about brains - specifically, how your brain looks and acts while you are sleeping.

It has been found that the brain will enter four different states while the body and mind are asleep. These four stages can be broken into two main categorical states: Non-Rapid Eye

Movement (NREM) and Rapid Eye Movement (REM).

During NREM, there is very little brain activity and movement as the brain transitions through the first three states of sleep.

In the first state, your body prepares itself for sleep. Your brain starts to quieten, and your heartbeat slows. You enter a state known as "dozing." Dozing occurs when you are coming to terms with the comfort of your bed, rolling the sheets in your fingers, and releasing heavy breaths of frustration because of all the things you didn't get to finish during the day.

Ninety minutes later, you should find yourself immersed in the second stage of sleep.

In this state, your brain is virtually empty, your body temperature is lowering, and your heart rate has slowed remarkably. The activity in your brain is almost non-existent, and mountains of melatonin are being secreted from your pineal gland into your blood, making you feel incredibly sleepy.

You might feel a flicker or two of muscle spasms as you drift off, perhaps waking you for a second before you relax and ease back into slumber. This is just the motor sensors in your brain becoming inhibited. This is known as a hypnic jerk and is believed to be an ancient warning used by our ancestors whenever they fell asleep climbing trees.

No one knows why we experience hypnic jerks, but that's my favorite guess so far.

During the third stage of sleep, every muscle and neuron in your body functions at its lowest potential. The brain is virtually inactive, save for a few tiny signals that are released to aid the brain in its recovery. Most meditations will play a frequency of zero to four Hz to endorse this state of sleep. To put that into perspective, the lowest note registered by humans is a B-flat on a bass guitar – a frequency of 35 Hz. No musical note is lower than that.

In other words, your brain is functioning at an exceptionally low frequency. During this stage of sleep, a hormone known as Gamma-aminobutyric acid (GABA) is released. GABA is an inhibitory transmitter, meaning that it prevents certain signals from entering the spinal column and the brain.

GABA acts like a girl's best friend at a party. If she doesn't think you are cool enough, you're not getting to her friend. Thus, GABA helps to increase positive mood and feelings within the body. She protects you from unwanted companions. Most people who wake immediately after this state will feel refreshed and well-rested.

Finally, after 90 minutes in each of the previous three states, the brain enters the fourth state of sleep. Strangely, this is where the brain begins to light back up again, and you enter the most vivid of dream states.

In this state, your body is completely paralyzed to keep you from acting out your dreams. Your cortex may be processing a series of random images or thoughts you had during the day or before you went to sleep. Your prefrontal cortex is asleep, meaning you won't be able to understand or make sense of any of the visuals, and your amygdala is wide awake. Your amygdala is where all your emotions and memories are processed. This means that, in sleep, it is not uncommon to see the faces of people you know or to feel very intense feelings and urges.

What do you do with your surreal dreams? Maybe you dreamt you were eating chocolate chip ice-cream in a crystal cave? What do you to make of that? Or should you not make anything of it? Surely, if this is your brain's way of healing after a long day, this image has a pivotal role to play in its recovery.

Except that isn't the case at all. Once the brain has finished its ninety minutes of frivolous activation, it reroutes back to stage one. During a good night's sleep, a person may cycle through these stages several times before they wake.

The Brain and Dreaming

You can dream during any of the four stages, but how you dream is different. During the first stage of sleep, as you are dozing off, you may experience some light hallucinogenic dreams. Perhaps you hear someone calling your name. Depending on the urgency in their voice, you may wake up or - like my mother - ignore it and yell back only if it doesn't stop calling.

What about whispers just before bed?

Relax - I doubt that there are any ghosts or ghouls in your home. You'd know if there were, and you'd be reading an entirely different book. If you're hearing whispers, it's another sign that your prefrontal cortex is shutting down while your cortex is still playing back new ideas or ancient tales told by old friends. If you told me you could understand these whispers, we would be having a different conversation.

During the second stage of sleep, your cortex ravages you with a series of words, thoughts, and ideas. Nothing is being played out, yet, and there is no storyline or context - just random fragments of thoughts. I'll give you an example: *The tiger runs farther than the rabbit. Perhaps there is a barbecue in its ear or lasagna for dessert.* These fragments don't make sense. They are passing thoughts, sounds, and ideas without meaning.

It is only in the third stage of sleep that your ideas and thoughts start to come alive. When I say come alive, I mean it. For many people, it is during the third stage that they experience night terrors or sleepwalking.

What are they experiencing?

For people with night terrors, their prefrontal cortex has woken up while the rest of their brain and body is still sound asleep. Their amygdala is working overtime as it plummets through all the thoughts and visuals that the cortex is throwing at it, leaving the paralyzed individual with a series of unanswered, and often terrifying, questions.

Think of it this way: you went to bed, but then woke up in a jungle filled with singing chipmunks and man-eating gorillas, yet you can't move or think clearly enough to remind yourself you are still in your bed and that these images aren't real. Sleep paralysis can be a frightening experience for many people, and often occurs in individuals with high levels of stress and anxiety.

For those who struggle with sleepwalking, the opposite happens. The prefrontal cortex remains asleep, but the motor inhibitors in the brain stop working, allowing the body to move. They aren't dreaming, so why are they moving? Remember that the amygdala and cortex are still working. They might be performing habitual behaviors. In some cases, sleepwalkers will move around objects in their homes. How can they do that if they are asleep? Is it their memory? Or can they see? If they could see, they would be able to register that they are out of bed. This leaves the most feasible explanation: They are acting out their ids. However, I suspect Freud may have been hinting at more alarming urges than cleaning the floors of one's home.

Finally, as the brain enters the REM stage, your mind is flooded with imagery and scenes mixed in with fragments of strange ideas you may have had in the previous stages, creating a vivid and strange dream experience. All this makes your regular bedtime routine seem like a trip to Disney World. There is so much happening in your brain when you sleep it is a wonder you can get any rest. Once the REM stage is complete, the brain cycles back to the first state.

Waking in a Dream

Waking up *in* a dream and waking *from* a dream are two very different things. Don't get it twisted. When you wake up in a dream, your mind becomes lucid, and your prefrontal cortex is activated, much like in the situation of night terrors.

Are night terrors and lucid dreaming not the same thing?

Good question. It's easy to assume that they are, but no. Lucid dreaming encourages a level of personal control that those plagued by night terrors are unable to harness. Lucid dreaming is the purposeful awakening of the prefrontal cortex, while night terrors are the unexpected or mistaken awakening.

Lucid dreaming is intentional and thus, when you wake in your dream, you may discover certain cues to help you navigate the real from the unreal. This technique is also very helpful for those suffering from nightmares. However, they only work once the mind and body have relaxed enough to concentrate on what is happening.

Once the mind and the body have settled, one may notice habitual signs of their dream world. Everyone's dreams are different and, therefore, the cues may differ from person to person.

For me, the dripping, moving pictures and the waving walls are things I have noticed in my dreams throughout my life. Having programmed my brain to pick up on those cues, the second I see them, I become aware that I am dreaming. Once I am aware that I am dreaming, I can change the events that are taking place.

For example, the worst nightmare I had was when I was ten

years old. In the dream, I had gotten lost with my sister in the school playground. As we searched for our parents, we accidentally stumbled across Pumpkinhead's room. He was asleep in the bed by my math teacher's desk. As we entered, I could hear his dreams warning us to leave or perish. I awoke with the voices still echoing in my head.

Had I understood the art of lucid dreaming at the time, the events may have gone as follows:

I had gotten lost with my sister in the school playground. We searched for our parents but couldn't find them. Then, we entered a bedroom.

Let me repeat that last phrase.

We entered a bedroom.

That should have been the first cue. Let's carry on, though, for fun.

Pumpkinhead was sleeping in the bed beside my math teacher's desk.

That's as imaginative as I'm going to get. There are no beds in math classes. And, if there were, you need to find the genius that managed to convince the math teacher to bring in this accessory.

By this point, I should have realized I was dreaming and reshaped my dream accordingly. A bed is not in this math class. Perhaps it is just a couch, and your parents are sitting there waiting for you so you can go home.

Cue relief and peace - it sounds easy, but it isn't.

Forgetting Versus Remembering

If everyone dreams, how come not all of us remember these experiences?

Again, this is something that has baffled scientists for centuries. First, why you dream at all is a mystery; and second, how are some people able to remember their dreams while others aren't? This is a question that has thousands of theories, but no real answers.

The first theory is that some people can remember with practice while some can't, no matter how many times they try. The second is that those who remember their dreams may have coincidentally just woken from one - making it easier to recall.

Remember that your amygdala plays a big part in how you process your dreams. With your amygdala also being responsible for your memories and emotions, it may just be that your amygdala wasn't stimulated by your dream. It may also be that you didn't dream at all during any of the stages.

Stats show that certain medications and ages tend to inhibit brain activity throughout the four stages of sleep, pressing the snooze button on all dreams.

Other studies show that people who live highly stressful lives or battle with anxiety are more likely to remember their dreams. This might be because there is too much stress in their bodies for the brain inhibitors to block.

Dreaming is still a mystery. No one knows why we do it, why some can remember their dreams, and why some can't.

Chapter 2

Why Dreaming Is Important

Psychological Introspection

Sigmund Freud believed that dreams were manifestations of our greatest sexual fears, desires, and anxieties. Furthermore, he suggested that dreams comprise our most taboo thoughts - so much so that the human mind cautiously disguises the meaning of the dream with ludicrous objects and images. Freud thought that the only way to understand the meaning of a dream was to analyze the objects within.

The humanistic approach suggests that dreams exist to better us. Humanists believe that what is most important about dreams is your reactions to, and within, them. How one behaves in the dream is of great significance. Analyzing this behavior can help you navigate real-life challenges.

Similarly, the behaviorist interpretation of dreams suggests that environmental stimulation guides the nature and performance of the dream. For example, if you are constantly being pushed by your employer to work hard and produce outstanding projects, you'll likely dream about being pushed. Understanding your dreams in contrast to your waking life helps you understand how to prevent the dream from reoccurring and reduces your real-life problems.

The cognitive approach suggests that dreams offer an opportunity to engage with feelings and thoughts you can't engage with during the day; especially when your days are flooded with activities. You might not even realize how stressed you are until bedtime, when your brain can finally work through the pain, flusters, and anger you experienced during the day.

What all these approaches have in common is that they all maintain that ignoring a dream is ignoring the self. Regardless of what the dream is, and no matter how nonsensical it may seem, ignoring it can create further challenges in your life and lead to impediments in self-confidence, self-respect, identity, and self-understanding.

It's like thinking, "I'm hungry - but that's not important."

When did, "I'm scared, stressed, tired, angry, and unhappy," stop mattering? You matter, and so do your dreams.

To heal yourself and grow as a person, you need to analyze your dreams. You can use the above approaches and theories interchangeably.

Think back to your last dream - what were some of the themes? Were you running from something? Were you looking out at the sunrise? What were you doing? How did you feel about it? Were you afraid? Were you in awe? How do you feel about it now?

When I was eighteen, I had a dream that I was surrounded by evil, strategic "merpeople."

I was underwater and, though I could breathe, I was afraid that the merpeople would not see me as one of them and would try to destroy me.

Some of the themes in my dream are water, mythical creatures, tribalism, and isolation.

The fear that I felt in the dream, and where the fear stemmed from, are important in understanding what was going on in my head. I wasn't afraid of drowning. I wasn't afraid of being incapable. I was afraid of not being able to fit in.

This is an understandable fear for anyone in their late teens, especially eighteen-year-olds as they face independence and the big world ahead of them.

Acknowledging what is happening is only one part of the process; the second part is physically dealing with that fear.

By understanding that I was afraid of not being accepted, I was also able to modulate that fear with the insight that not everyone is going to like me. As long as I like myself, that is enough to get by.

Trauma

For people battling with trauma or post-traumatic stress disorder (PTSD), remembering and interpreting dreams can be a helpful addition to their recovery plan.

There is a sad misconception that only war veterans or victims of physical abuse can claim to have suffered trauma. This is untrue. Trauma can be a consequence of anything: a car accident, a few unkind words thrown in passing, stress, or tragic events such as the loss of a family member.

PTSD is categorized by the existence of at least two of the following symptoms:

- Nightmares

- Vivid memories

- Hypervigilance

- Emotional and physical outbursts

- Startled responses

- Difficulty concentrating

Off the top of my head, I know three friends who could be officially diagnosed with PTSD but aren't. A study by Aco Staff in 2021 found that nearly 17% of all college students are suffering from PTSD (*How lucid dreams cure PTSD, phobias, nightmares, and emotional trauma*, 2018).

With these statistics and the world's fast pace, it is no wonder that there's a rising interest in dreaming.

You can use lucid dreams to treat PTSD and trauma by using the principles of exposure therapy. Exposure therapy works by slowly exposing a person to their greatest fears in a safe and controlled environment.

If you are afraid of spiders, you can overcome this fear by gently exposing yourself to them in a lucid dream. Being able to control where and how you interact with your fears can do wonders for your self-esteem and ability to process your fears.

For example, you might enter your dream, become lucid, and then interact with your environment to alleviate your fear of spiders. You might conjure a giant spider and give it a funny hat or purple kitten heels. You may give the spider a personality. You'll develop a relationship with the creature and, as best friends, you will tour the galaxy together. Such an interactive and compassionate dream is bound to change your perception of spiders. When you have this dream multiple times, you train your brain to see spiders differently. You begin to accept and appreciate them.

The same idea applies to dealing with trauma. First, it is important to understand what your trauma is. Trauma isn't depression; it has a specific onset, one that can be acknowledged through subconscious thoughts, fears, feelings, and dreams. Once you know what your trauma is, you can begin to deal with it.

Let's analyze the context around my mermaid dream to help you better understand how to heal your trauma within your dreams.

When I was 18, I was being bullied in school. My dream of being chased by unfriendly mermaids represents my trauma and feelings of isolation.

I could have the same dream every night, but that isn't going to do me any good. Rather, I'm going to change how the events in the dream unravel. I'm going to extend the dream and apply a more compassionate ending.

Before I can do this, I have to plan beyond what has happened. Ending my nightmare with me being enslaved by the mermaids isn't going to help my trauma. What might help my trauma is an ending I wanted in real life. Perhaps, at the end of my dream, I am accepted by the mermaids, or I exact my revenge on them.

The question I need to ask is, "What do I want?"

The answer may be very different for you, and that's okay. You need to choose what helps you sleep at night.

I have a rather fiery nature, and I do love a good battle scene that ends in victory. So, I opted to end my dream with me finding my place amidst an army of orcas. Together, we returned to the cave of mermaids and exacted our revenge. The mermaids retreated, and the orcas and I lived out the rest of our days with respect for one another.

Revisiting this dream and extending it in this way helped me understand who I am. Now, I can accept that I hate how some people treated me, and I want them to see that I am happy without them. I understand that not everything about me is light and happy. I can feel happy after getting revenge, and that is okay. That is human.

However, that acceptance can only come from opening your heart and mind to who you are - the "true you" found during your most unconscious state.

I go to sleep accepting the ending I have constructed. I dream it, control it, and it happens. My nightmare has become a wonderful dream of heroism. That victory doesn't only affect me in my sleep but during my waking life, too.

Now, I can begin my recovery knowing that I am not a weak, lost, young woman that everyone hates. Instead, I am a strong individual who knows she has value and can do anything she sets her mind to. I have a place I belong, I have friends, and I'm important.

Dr. Stephen Aizenstat developed this practice of analyzing and extending dreams to help alleviate symptoms in trauma survivors (De Borde, 2019). It's a phenomenal and empowering technique that aims to help people reimagine their lives and restructure their paths. It enables trauma survivors to play the producer and commander of their own lives rather than the victim. I refuse to be the victim in someone else's dream anymore - join me.

Ideas and Success

There are hundreds of well-known businessmen, scientists, and millionaires who started their renowned journeys after one remembered dream.

Notorious horror writer Stephen King claimed that many of his works were merely scripts stemming from his dreams. In his interviews, he states with grueling detail how he used his dreams as a source of inspiration for his books. I won't burden you with the details, but it fits.

World-renowned electro-musician Richard D. James would replicate the sounds he heard in his dreams and mix them into his albums. His music has made him millions.

Einstein could be the most renowned dreamer of our time. Many of his theories are largely based on the questions he posed as he reflected on his dreams. His theory of relativity originally stemmed from a dream he had about cows jumping over a fence (SVAdmin, 2021).

How often have you found yourself lying in bed at night counting sheep or cows or pigs as they hopped over a little bale of hay?

Einstein didn't accept the scene as meaningless. Instead, he pondered over how each of the cows viewed that same scene differently and why. Thus, the theory of relativity was born.

These individuals used their dreams to inspire their successes. It's interesting to think that your future is just waiting on you to remember one dream.

Lucid dreaming isn't just about creating new ideas. Lucid dreaming grants the skill of setting a goal and achieving it. The whole concept of the activity is to plan and set forth. When you enter a dream and become lucid, your first task is to exert some form of control in the dream - whether it's choosing the color of the sky or walking a few steps in a certain direction. Sometimes the plan is grand, like alleviating trauma, understanding yourself more, writing a book, or solving a math problem. Lucid dreams allow you to accomplish a task and, often, you will. You accomplish these tasks because you are in control.

Imagine how it would feel to repeatedly conquer your goals. You wouldn't just become a better planner; you would become more confident, your sense of self-worth would grow, your ideas would become grander, and you'd feel more fulfilled.

You might remember a small part of your dream, just like Stephen King, but the courage to pursue that dream - to enhance and extend it and share it with the world - can only come from a practiced dreamer. Stephen King, Richard James, and Albert Einstein were well-practiced lucid dreamers. Being so well-practiced helped them find the courage to stand up for what they believed in and wanted, and to take a hold of their future. They let their dream worlds empower their everyday life.

This is how lucid dreaming can help you become successful.

CHAPTER 3

What Is Lucid Dreaming?

History

Lucid dreaming has a long and complex history going back thousands of years, before the birth of Christ. The first documented lucid dreaming event was found in the *Hindu Tract* and later transcribed in the *Tibetan Book of the Dead* (Hurd, 2022).

It worth noting that lucid dreaming was practiced long before it was written about. Many African tribes tell old stories of how kings and queens were visited by their ancestors in dreams. Egyptians were known to analyze their dreams and use symbols and signs to understand their meaning.

There was so much cultural merging along the Nile routes of Ancient Africa between the Muslims, Bantu, Canaanites, Pygmies, Portuguese, and Romans that there is no telling where or how the practice originated.

In Egypt and many other African capitals, lucid dreams were believed to be messages sent by the gods to predict the future. In some central African capitals, lucid dreams were gifts of wisdom or creativity, bestowed upon a chosen few. In Tibet and India, lucid dreams were a prescription for healing. In ancient Greece, lucid dreams held no more significance than dreams themselves.

With everything that science has shown us today, these historical beliefs are no more right than wrong. The truth lies in what you believe. Power comes from what you believe has power. If you can find meaning in your dreams, you give your dreams the power to influence your life.

However, it all starts with the right mindset. If you don't believe that dreams have meaning, regardless of their place in science and religious communities, you'll never remember your dreams. Similarly, if you constantly believe that your nightmares are too harrowing to connect with, you will never relieve yourself of them, you'll never grow, and you'll never be free.

You must acknowledge that dreaming has the potential to change your life. If you believe that your dreams can help you see the future, they will. If you believe that they can help you be successful, they will. But you have to believe with every fiber of your being. The potential of your dreams is only limited by you.

The Science

Lucid dreaming was not accepted in the scientific community until 1978, despite the number of people and cultures claiming its existence and benefits (kzt5196, 2015).

The first plausible account was considered by Cecilia Green in the 1960s in her study on false awakenings. However, the first bit of scientific proof was obtained in 1975 when Keith Hearne, a renowned researcher of psychic phenomena, noticed the eye of a volunteer twitch while they were asleep (kzt5196, 2015).

False awakenings and eye twitches revealed that, while asleep, the volunteers were conscious enough to feel the effects of their dreams and react to them. This phenomenon of the prefrontal cortex being awake during sleep had never been witnessed, analyzed, or explained by a practitioner. The findings startled the community and saw numerous studies trying to expand into the realm of lucid dreaming.

But the real proof wasn't found by analyzing people. What if I told you that most studies that proved the existence of lucid dreaming were done on cats? Yes, cats! Using EEGs, MRIs, and EOGs, scientists were able to scan and analyze the workings of cats' brains within the different stages of sleep. These scans proved that the prefrontal cortex of the brain was still active during sleep.

So, the next time you joke about your cat wanting to kill you in your sleep, know that it might be one of their recurring lucid dreams, where they are fully conscious and aware of their actions. The same scans were done on humans a few years later and the results were identical. People, like cats, can become conscious in their dreams, and in doing so, control them.

How It Works

For you to become lucid in a dream, you need to become aware that you are dreaming by switching on your prefrontal cortex.

How can you do this if lucid dreaming is only possible in the fourth sleep state when much of your brain isn't working?

There are a variety of methods that can be used to wake your prefrontal cortex. The first is to say a few affirmations before you go to bed, confirming with your mind and your body that you will participate in the act of lucid dreaming. Do you remember Gabba, the gatekeeper in your brain that acts like the girl at the party? Gabba is released by the reticular activating system in your brain, RAS. By affirming what you want to do, the RAS will limit the influence Gabba has on the information entering your mind and you'll be able to think a little more clearly.

Sound too good to be true?

Think of it this way: Have you ever tried to get your body to wake up on its own without using an alarm clock? By simply telling your body to get up at a certain time, your body clock, along with the RAS in your brain, allow you to wake up at the same time every day. The alarm is just an invention crafted by anxious people. Lucid dreaming affirmations work the same way.

Another method is analyzing realistic and non-realistic environments. Watch any new animation and try to describe the parts that are realistically impossible and the parts that could be viewed as realistic. Does the pig fly in the movie? Is that possible in reality? Can rabbits paint rooms blue? Do blue rooms exist? You can easily sense whether you are in a dream or not by practicing differentiating dreams from reality. If pigs are flying, you're dreaming; but if the room is blue, you might not be.

Being able to differentiate a dream from reality can be a tricky thing, especially when you don't have access to the logical reasoning center right away. Rest assured, the more you practice, the easier it will get and the faster your prefrontal cortex will wake.

If you want the main entertainment now, without having to murk through the hows and whos, you can try listening to frequencies between 25 and 40 Hz. These frequencies, associated with the second and third stages of sleep, force the prefrontal cortex to remain active as the rest of the brain and body fall into slumber.

Lastly, there are also devices that you can buy or make to help you identify when you are sleeping. The Sound Oasis Mask presents a series of pictures that slowly lighten or darken, depending on your sleeping schedule. As you doze off, the mask presents a darkening picture of sunsets. As you wake, the mask presents a brightening picture of a sunrise. Through the night, you can set small light flickering. These flickers won't be bright enough to wake you, but you'll be able to identify them while in your dream state. By identifying them in your dream state, you are also able to identify that you are asleep.

The same idea applies to setting a light bulb to go off at a particular time or getting your phone to sound a low alarm at a certain hour. It would be best to set an alarm or light to go off a few hours before you are due to wake up. Then, switch it off and fall back asleep. The results may fascinate you.

Types of Lucid Dreams

Wake Initiated

Scientists have theorized that there are two different types of lucid dreams. Wake-initiated lucid dreams (WILDs) manifest when continuous reflective thoughts are experienced while falling asleep.

WILD dreams are very difficult to initiate because you have to keep your mind conscious as you fall asleep. Thinking clearly and sleeping are two opposite activities. Have you ever tried to think rationally while drunk or exhausted? It's almost impossible. But every once in a while, something important will get your adrenaline going and you can focus on what needs to be done.

WILD dreams work the same way. You have to want it badly enough and practice. One day, when your mind is strong enough, you will experience it for yourself and feel even more powerful because of it.

WILD dreams are conscious, focused, planned, and forced experiences in lucid dreaming. It takes an exceptionally well-practiced dreamer to initiate a lucid dream immediately after falling asleep.

This is a skill you want if you plan to take control of your life. Being able to slip easily in and out of wakefulness and lucid dreaming is hugely beneficial. If you can control your mind to such an extent, imagine what else you can accomplish.

I'll tell you the story of my first WILD dream. It was a Sunday, five years after the retreat. I'd gone to church with my mother, not something I did regularly, but it made her happy, so I joined her.

Afterward, when we went home, we had a big Sunday lunch. Throughout my life, my mother has made a big meal on Sunday afternoons.

So I ate well and, with a belly uncomfortably full, I went to lie down.

While I was looking up at her old, broken ceiling from the mattress on the living room floor, I couldn't help but reflect on all the broken roofs I had slept under.

And so, I decided to slip into a dream, fly onto the roof, and fix it. I kept my focus on my goal.

Almost instantly I slipped from my body. I was like a ghost attached by a rope to my sleeping form below. With my nose poking toward the sky, I flew up and out through the ceiling. Above our roof and surrounded by fluffy white clouds, I looked at my hands, focusing all my intent, love, and care on them.

I placed my palms on the roof and forced the tiles to multiply and cover the holes. It felt like something inside of me was being pushed out. Like something from my very core was being pulled by a rope into the open sky and fitted to our broken roof.

Slowly, the hole closed, and I floated back toward my body.

As I awoke, I knew things were about to change.

The following week, a house with three rooms in a good neighborhood was put up for sale at a shockingly low price. I put down a small deposit and, by some stroke of magic, I got it.

I'd found the courage in my dream to take the next step. I believed I could fix things, and so I did. That is the power of a WILD dream.

Dream Initiated

Dream-initiated lucid dreams (DILDs) are spontaneous. DILD dreams aren't manifested through control and focus. They may have been planned, but they aren't forced like WILD dreams. You don't need a strong, focused mind to experience a DILD dream. But your mind must be open to the world, new experiences, and new possibilities.

Around 80% of lucid dreams are DILD dreams ("2 different types," n.d.).

One way to know that you are having a DILD dream is if you have to think about it. If you aren't sure or have to be guided by small cues to acknowledge you are dreaming, then you are experiencing a DILD dream.

When you experience WILD dreams, you know instantly where you are headed. With a DILD dream, however, you only know you are dreaming during the dream.

In the DILD dream, you slowly become conscious of the absurdity of the dream. You find yourself focusing on objects, situations, writings, and images. Nothing in a dream is fixed. Things are always warped and moving. So, if you can center yourself for a moment and focus on one thing, you will bring yourself to lucidity.

This realization that you are dreaming makes you an observer, a participant, and the director of your dream. You're no longer a fumbling, mumbling actor on autopilot or following someone else's plan. Instead, you become strong, unyielding, and brave.

I'll give you an example of a DILD dream I had when I started practicing lucid dreaming.

It was just a few months after the retreat. A family member had tragically passed away and I was desperate to feel that sense of control and power again. I wanted to see them. I wanted to dream of them and know I was dreaming so that I could say goodbye.

Every day, I sat in a circle of pretty stones I made trying to initiate a WILD dream so I could speak to my loved one. I didn't work. No matter how hard I prayed, begged, or studied, nothing worked.

One day, I decided I was tired of trying. I closed my eyes with solemn regret and went to sleep - not for any other purpose than to rest.

And that's when it happened.

I was still lying on my mattress, but I wasn't supposed to know that. I was supposed to be asleep and, if I wasn't, I wanted to get up - except I couldn't find the strength in my arms to push me to my feet.

I tried to kick, shout, or move. Because of the struggle, I

tumbled sideways off my mattress and onto the floor. The tumble startled me. The need to be away from the floor filled my mind and I lifted (floated) above the floor.

That's when I knew I was dreaming.

I tested this new flying ability around the living room, straight through a mirror.

In the mirror, I saw some hellish things I won't speak of, but I made it to another side filled with golden chrysanthemums, my departed loved one's favorite flower.

I flew through the field and glided through the blue sky and white clouds, until below me I saw them walking happily through the field, carrying a basket of flowers. I didn't call out. I don't know why I didn't, but I think I figured they were busy. Seeing them happy and alright was all I needed. I didn't want to disturb their rest, and I no longer needed to disturb mine.

I imagined myself back in my body and poof: There I was.

I startled awake, breathing heavily - I did fall off my mattress. That only made the experience more real.

Lucid dreaming allowed me to find closure, move on, and find peace. DILD dreams are as precious and rewarding as WILD dreams. Without them, there is no concept of lucid dreaming at all, no means to practice, and no way to take control of your mind and life.

PART 2

What You Need to Lucid Dream

Before you attempt to run a marathon, you must learn to walk first, right?

Lucid dreaming is the same. You need to engage with smaller practices and mental understanding before attempting the big stuff. This doesn't mean you can't try the more intimidating exercises; try them. However, acknowledge why they might tire you and why they might not work.

Before falling perfectly into a WILD dream, you need to understand and engage with lucid dreaming while awake. Knowing how to relax and slip out of reality is one of the first things you should familiarize yourself with.

The hypnagogia technique, limb-by-limb method, the Salvadore Dali way, and the talking approach are all amazing methods that will help you navigate the challenges of inducing a lucid dream.

As you progress through your exercises and practices, you'll advance through the five stages of lucid dreaming.

In each stage, you'll discover a new element of yourself, delve deeper into the dreaming world, ask questions, and find answers to questions you never thought you would. You'll push barriers and fight limitations - and everything you find in your dreams will inspire you in your wake life. You'll eventually become a strong, brave, and unyielding individual who can not only accomplish anything they set their mind to, but who is wise, compassionate, understanding, knowledgeable, observant, and kind.

CHAPTER 4

How to Fall Asleep Consciously

Lucid Hypnagogia Technique

A hypnagogic state is a miraculous, hallucinogenic sensory experience that occurs just as you fall asleep. Once you understand it and become familiar with it, you will recognize it every time it occurs. Becoming familiar with this state is vital in inducing wake dreams. By remaining aware while being lulled to sleep, you can shape your visions and desires to lead you into the lucid dreaming landscape of your choice.

The hypnagogic state usually begins with blobs of purple and green luminescent colors flashing in the darkness of your closed eyes. From experiencing these colors, you may experience various visions, sounds, sensations, and thoughts as you travel down the path toward sleep. These sensory experiences are tangible. If you focus hard enough on them, you can manipulate them to appear how you'd like.

Close your eyes and cover them with the palms of your hands. Breathe deeply and stay focused on trying to see through your eyelids, as if you are looking into the distance. What do you see? Do you see shapes, forms, and colors? It's almost like a warping, geometrical painting. Reds, blues, and greens should all stand out for you.

It's not magic; it's science. *Fovea centralis* is a collection of tiny cones and rods at the back of our eyes that react to light and help us see colors. Our eyes are programmed to see black, white, red, green, and blue. In different lighting, the cones and rods may combine to form pinks, purples, and yellows. If you are color-blind, you have a unique proportion of cones and rods at the back of your eyes, making you see colors differently.

At this moment, with your hands over your eyes, get used to your geometric patterns. They are as beautiful and unique as you are. Remember them and allow yourself to engage with them as often as you like. Familiarize yourself with them so that, while you are falling asleep, you can recognize what is happening and you can remain lucid.

Once you are familiar with this state of being, you can try to manipulate it to induce a lucid dream.

I want you to find a darkened room and lie down as if you are getting ready to fall asleep. Close your eyes, but observe the darkness beyond. Breathe deeply and relax your body. Quieten your mind through meditation and allow yourself to become conscious of your feelings, passing thoughts, and environment. How do you feel? What do you smell? Are you hungry? Are you sad? Recognize these feelings and let them go.

Slowly the geometrical patterns will emerge, becoming brighter and brighter. Play with these pictures, visualize new ones, and incorporate old ones. Try to tell a story with the patterns, elicit memories, and conjure people or places.

Eventually, sleep will overcome you and your dreaming mind will take control; instantly you will find yourself conscious in the realm of the unconscious - in a world you created. The whole process should take no more than an hour.

It may take you a few tries to get this right. Remember to remain calm and relaxed. Even though you are forcing a lucid dream, you aren't forcing yourself to sleep. The idea is to allow your mind to latch onto the dream and control it while willing yourself to sleep. That is tricky, especially if you are excited about this practice. Stay calm; it will happen when it happens.

There is only so much you can control right now. Nothing

happens in a day. Let yourself practice the phenomenon so that you can be grateful for conquering the perceivably impossible when you are finally successful. If you get it right straight away, there is little to be proud of. Give yourself a chance to be proud of your effort, creativity, and courage.

Limb-by-Limb Relaxation

Jacobson's relaxation technique, or limb-by-limb relaxation (LBLR), is a sleep therapy technique that involves tightening and relaxing your muscles in specific patterns. The goal is to release tension from your muscles while keeping your mind focused and conscious of the tension in your body - and on your goals and desires. The art of tensing and releasing muscles relaxes the body and mind.

Find a quiet space to rest. Begin by wrinkling your forehead. Lift your eyebrows and close your eyes as tight as you can. Create as much tension in your face as you can. Hold this position, then slowly relax every part of your face. Release your jaw, feel your cheeks fall, and let your eyes droop.

Once you're done with your face, tense your arms, your shoulders, and fingers. Curl your arms around your torso and hug yourself as tight as possible. Give yourself that wonderful, warm, and appreciative hug you've been holding back. Breathe in and hold that position. As you exhale, let your arms fall to your sides and allow your fingers to open wide.

Next is your chest - breathe in deeply and allow air to stream into your belly. Squeeze the air inside of you by tightening your chest and abdomen. Slowly exhale and allow the air to seep out of you. Acknowledge how your breath feels. Is it warm, cold, jagged, or smooth? Don't try to change it; just become aware of it.

I want you to squeeze your buttocks, thighs, and hips. You should feel your skin come together in a firm, tight heap. Afterward, tighten your toes and curl them inwards, then flex your calves and stretch out your legs. One by one, release your toes, calves, thighs, and buttocks.

Lastly, tense the muscles in your back. Curve your spine outwards as if you are folding in on yourself. Breathe deeply and hold this position. When you are ready, relax your muscles and allow your back to straighten against the surface you're lying on.

By now, you should feel as if you are sinking deeper and deeper into the dream world. Allow yourself a few last-minute thoughts. Get comfortable and prepare for a lucid dream.

As you are dozing, plan where you aim to end up. Imagine the setting and play with the little shards of light as they reflect behind your eyes. As you fall into slumber, your mind will be conscious enough to explore your dream world.

LBLR helps with more than just inducing lucid dreams. It's recommended by cognitive behavioral therapists because of its potential in aiding with stress relief and panic attacks. LBLR has also been found to reduce blood pressure, slow heart rate, and reduce fatigue, muscle pain, anxiety, and depression. Incorporating LBLR will certainly leave you feeling happier and healthier.

The benefits of lucid dreaming, combined with LBLR, create a heightened sense of pleasure that empowers and restores you. Together, these two practices can help you become the person you always hoped to be.

But remember, every practice takes time. Don't expect to feel the changes after the first try. Experience the journey, explore your options, and enjoy the process.

Lucid Slumber with a Key

Salvador Dali rarely slept - which perhaps explains some of his more questionable ideas, as well as his most complicated and profound ones. Instead of resting, Salvador would escape into the realm of lucid dreams as often as he could. As he was preparing for sleep, he would settle in a chair situated above a metal plate. He would hold a heavy metal key in his hands which, as he was dozing off, would fall and clatter against the metal plate on the floor. Dali would wake, but not completely. His consciousness would awaken within his dream and allow him to grapple with challenging theories and ideas.

Imagine being able to enter the dream of Salvador Dali. What peculiarities would you see? What strange entities would lurk about, and what objects would move and communicate? What would they tell you?

Salvador Dali was so taken by his world of dreams that he longed to bring them into his waking life. His nighttime ideas led to the theory of surrealism. Surrealism became a worldwide movement within the art, music, and theater spaces in the 1920s (History.com Editors, 2018). The movement aimed to explore the realm of dreams, the peculiar, and the impossible within the waking world. Paintings of purple lakes and yellow skies lined the walls of the elitists. Music depicting nighttime strolls in abandoned buildings filled every restaurant in town. Theater productions told strange tales of monster rabbits and moving beds.

Who better to inspire our dream practice world than the man who brought dreams to life?

Start by practicing Salvador's technique while you're awake. Sit comfortably in a quiet, dark room and, just like Salvador, find something of weight to hold. It can be anything from a book to a heavy necklace, or even a shoe. Allow yourself to relax. Meditate, breathe in deeply, and acknowledge your secondary thoughts. Let them slip away like the object in your hands. As you fall asleep, let the object in your hand drop. In those split seconds as the object crashes to the floor, become aware of the visions in your mind.

When it hits the ground, wake up, grab a pen and paper, and write down your experience. Describe your experience in as much detail as possible. Once you've done this, analyze it. What do the images tell you about yourself? Why do you think you saw what you saw? How do you think your visions can help you?

Practice this exercise as often as you like until you can slip in and out of a lucid dream quickly and without struggle.

When you're ready, prepare yourself to perform this exercise at bedtime.

Grab something of weight just before going to bed. Find an item that has a different texture from the items on your bed.

Hold this item close to your chest as you doze off. As you are falling asleep, remain conscious of how the object feels in your hands. As your muscles relax and twitch, your mind will be reminded of your purpose. You will awaken in your dream and be able to explore your mind fully.

Of course, it's important to remind you that losing sleep in pursuit of lucid dreaming defeats the point of this book. You cannot find yourself or achieve your goals if you are tired, ill, or frustrated. You need to sleep. Lucid dreaming should not impede this. Lucid dreaming should leave you feeling well-rested. If not, you might be too conscious in your sleep. So, attempt these exercises as much as your mind and body will allow. If you are battling to stay awake, sleep. Don't force yourself to stay awake to have a dream. Chances are, you will be too tired to remember it. Sleep when you need to, and practice when you feel strong. You have your whole life to get this right. Everyone finds their way when the time is right. No one can answer when that is. If we knew, we'd all be successful brilliant people. Just wait, be patient, and you will get it eventually.

Talk Yourself to Sleep

We all use an internal voice in our thinking process. We use this voice to acknowledge and confront our behavior, feelings, decisions, plans, and conversations. For example, when preparing for a speech, you might rehearse your words in your head. Or, when you're studying, you might run the information through your head. The voice you hear when participating in these activities is your internal voice.

The tone, location, and feel of this voice are very important in these activities. These traits control how we perceive ourselves and the world around us. For example, when you were first learning to drive, calling yourself and other drivers "idiots" in your head wasn't helpful. Calling them so, outside your mind, was even less so. All that tone of voice does is rile you up, making you feel angry and frustrated. It's like having a person yelling at you from the passenger seat. It's distracting and doesn't help you think clearly.

Of course, as you are dozing off, you need to stay clear of that angry driver tone. Rather, you should use the voice you used on the day that you felt broken but still managed to get yourself back up. That's the voice you want for this exercise.

It's a voice that is forgiving, kind, and compassionate. It's understanding; it isn't stern. It's unyielding - because it won't let you give up. Next time you hear your inner voice, gently redirect your thoughts to employ a more compassionate tone.

When you think "I need to get into the car right now or I'm going to be late again," tell your inner voice to change and start again:

"I should get in the car now, but I also need to deal with this task and calm down before driving. I am going to be late for work, but that does not reduce my worth."

You will feel calmer, and when you're calm, you can act fast and with more consideration for your situation and surroundings. When you panic and think angrily, you will stutter and stumble.

Once you can control your inner voice, you're ready to talk yourself to sleep. Lie down in your bed and get comfortable. Close your eyes and breathe deeply. Gently, talk yourself to sleep. Give yourself a reason to believe in yourself, your dreams, and the act of sleeping. Forgive yourself for the day's mistakes and let go of any negative thoughts or feelings you might have. You can use affirmations, poems, and motivational speeches to lull yourself into the realm of dreams.

Talking yourself to sleep is a great way to keep your brain conscious. As you enter the dream world, your inner voice will wake you up and remind you of your purpose.

CHAPTER 5

Tips and Strategies

Like most skills, you get better at lucid dreaming the more you practice. But, if you're a beginner, it can be intimidating to pursue a task you know little about. So, I'll give you a few pointers to get you started.

Sleep Hygiene

Good sleep hygiene is essential for peaceful sleep and lucid dreaming. Feeling dirty is bound to disrupt your sleep, so be sure to take the time to wash your face and body before bed. Although a warm bath is preferable because it soothes the soul, burns calories, and endorses dopamine and happy feelings, you can get the same effect with a cold shower, or a bucket of water and a cloth.

When I was growing up, we would often experience water outages. We would buy water from the store, boil it in the kettle, and have a nice hot bucket bath with a cloth and sponge. Although not ideal, it did make me feel cleaner than any shower. Maybe because I would scrub my skin a little more than if I was in the shower, in an attempt to ensure that I was clean. I would sleep so well on those long summer nights.

Along with being clean, ensure that the room is dark. Studies have found that a little light in the room can induce nightmares and leave one feeling fatigued. You can use a blackout curtain or an eye mask to make the room as dark as possible.

Next, try to ensure your sleeping chambers are as quiet as possible. Of course, living in New York, I know how difficult that can be, so be sure to invest in earplugs.

Screens and Information Consumption

Avoid looking at television or computer screens before bed. If you must, ensure you use nighttime lighting settings. These settings usually feature an orange hue on your device, which is better for you than electronic blue light. Blue lights keep your mind active for hours into the night.

The same goes for complex theoretical materials, studies, and horror stories. No murder mysteries before bedtime, no matter how thrilling. Rather, if you're adamant about reading a book before bed, ensure it's a meaningless pack of words that does nothing but relax you.

If you do read something complex before bed that leaves you feeling more alert, get up and go for a walk. Get a glass of water and think through what you need to do. Then, when you tire, climb back into bed and try to fall asleep.

Here's an interesting tip to help you. A study found that people who frequently played video games reported experiencing lucid dreams more often than those who didn't (James, 2021b). Video games allow the players the opportunity to control a character beyond themselves.

Sound familiar?

It should; that's what happens in a lucid dream. If you can control an on-screen character, you'll find the confidence to control the characters in your dreams, and in your own life. If it's possible, find time during the day to play a video game on your phone, Xbox, PSP, or computer.

Meditation and Relaxation

Meditation is an important skill, whether you believe it benefits you or not. You should practice it before bed if you intend on lucid dreaming. Breathe in deep and channel your air to your belly, then slowly exhale and become aware of how your breath feels. Allow all secondary thoughts to slip from your mind - don't focus on them, just let them pass. As you begin to relax, become aware of the space around you, as well as how you feel within it. Continue to breathe in and out until your mind begins to feel sleepy.

Diet

Your diet also plays a part in controlling your sleep. If possible, ensure that you drink and eat at least three to four hours before bed. Too much food and water can reduce the quality of your sleep - sugars and vitamins in food keep you active, and water plays a vital role of keeping you energized. When you eat and drink, your body processes these nutrients into the bloodstream, which circulates through your organs and energizes your body. It won't be easy to get restful sleep after eating a four-course meal before bed. Although some people feel sleepy after a heavy meal, that sleep is often restless.

One small glass of water is all you need to get you through the night. Anything more than that will keep you up.

And, while you're controlling your eating habits, prioritize foods rich in vitamin B6 or tryptophan, as these nutrients help induce lucid dreams. Some foods rich in B6 include bananas, potatoes, avocados, chicken, fish, pork, and tofu. Foods rich in tryptophan include yogurt, cheese, oats, dates, and chocolate.

Foods rich in B6 and tryptophan help our bodies make serotonin, which is responsible for our happy feelings. If you're feeling sad or depressed - or suffer from ADHD, anxiety, or autism - these foods can leave you feeling a little better about yourself. Being positive is essential when learning anything new, especially when you're trying to be successful.

If you are eating well but still can't lucid dream, try a lucid dreaming supplement. Acetylcholine is a chemical in the brain that helps send messages from one neuron to another. It also helps us progress through the sleeping stages. Scientists have found that acetylcholine is essential in inducing sleep, dreaming, learning, and memory recall.

There aren't foods with acetylcholine in it; instead, certain foods contain some of the building blocks needed to make this chemical. To increase the level of acetylcholine in your body, you can take choline bitartrate: a type of supplement. In doing so, your ability to recall dreams and remain conscious while asleep will improve.

CHAPTER 6

Five Stages of Lucid Dreaming

The goals, intent, and desires of a lucid dreamer define whether they are a beginner or not. Lucid dreaming expertise is built on the complexity of ideas, goals, and intent. Once you have elicited a lucid dream, depending on how advanced you are, the dreams vary in length, vividness, sense of control, and interaction within the dream landscape.

Pleasure and Pain Avoidance

As I began practicing lucid dreaming, I would seek out all the things I couldn't do in the real world like flying, eating cake, and visiting fabulous places like Paris. I would fly around and munch on delicious slices of chocolate cake with cream cheese frosting, while looking out at the Eiffel tower. There were no gutters (in my version of France), no pain, and no troubles - it was a perfect world.

As a novice lucid dreamer, you'll frequently find yourself immersed in the pleasure of the dream landscape, frequently ignoring the negative and painful elements within your mind. This is okay. Explore the positives as much as you can and be grateful, because it was your mind that created these beautiful sensations and images. You are wonderful and magical, and you should appreciate that about yourself.

But don't be afraid of the darkness beyond. Even though you're not ready to venture near it, acknowledge that it still exists. Living in bliss doesn't eradicate it. Instead, ride that pleasure and allow it to boost your confidence, self-awareness, and appreciation of your mind. Then, use these boosts to prepare yourself for the battle against your darker side.

Manipulation and Movement

The second stage in a lucid dreamer's journey is like the first. In this stage, you are still trying to experience pleasure and avoid pain, but you begin to gain more control over your character and world. You develop the ability to shift and reshape scenes, objects, and people. You can prolong your dream and journey a little further. You become capable of recognizing goals within your dream and can follow them to varying extents. Although you might quickly awaken from your dream, you have the potential to keep yourself in the dream longer than in stage one.

Power, Purpose, and Primacy

With a little more experience, as you enter the third stage, you will be able to interpret the dream landscape as your canvas - where you can paint and explore whatever you like. You will find the potential for experiences in any given scenario. You have the ability and the openness to travel from a wedding to a shopping center within the same scene. Nothing in your dream is off limits; just like in life, anything is possible.

Within this stage, your desire to find pleasure is no longer your primary objective. At this stage, you develop the potential and desire to push boundaries and limits. You begin to wonder about what you are capable of, how much you can remember, and how much more you can achieve.

Now, you are more goal oriented. You know what you want and are willing to work hard to get it.

You are willing to conquer the negative thoughts; ready to interrogate them, confront them, bully them, and wipe them out. You're ready to explore why they existed in the first place and find alternatives, new endings, new ideas, and replacement thoughts.

It's during this stage that you will uncover your true self.

Reflection, Reaching Out, and Wonder

This is a particularly enchanting stage. You have surpassed your ideas of limitations and grown from your experiences.

What more is there to learn?

If you're asking this in your dream, you are at the fourth stage. At this stage, it's all about exploring your subconscious and speaking to a higher power.

- "Who am I?"

- "Is this dream part of me?"

- "What does any of this mean?"

Imagine having the reasons for your dreams answered within

the dream itself. That's what happens at this stage. Answers are handed to you, on a silver plate, by you.

Having access to such complex answers while asleep makes you appreciate yourself more when awake - because you already had all the answers. You know as much as you need to. But, when we don't take care of ourselves, when we stop listening to our minds and bodies, we become deaf to what we have to say. We ignore the truth. We embody the lies that society has invented about us: that we are lazy, grumpy, stupid, arrogant, cocky, or overly sensitive.

These are observations, and they may be right, but there is always more to it. You are these things, sometimes, and you are others at other times. Our knowledge of ourselves is complicated and we can't possibly understand it with a rational mind.

We need our dream landscape to help us navigate the implausible, the insane, the quirky, and the unimaginable. What if you're not overly sensitive, but an empath? What if you aren't just picking up on your own emotions, but those of others, and those that came before them: their past loved ones, their pets, and the terrors they faced? What if you have a gift for sensing those who have passed? What if your gift is because of a genetic mutation?

What if your depression is because of an experience you had before your brain could form enough connections to remember anything?

None of this is easily conceivable when awake and rational. You need to lift the barrier of rationality to explore your whole truth: a truth you already own, but don't have access to.

By uncovering this truth in your dream, you allow your wake self the same ability. After that, you're unstoppable. Nothing is more powerful than knowing who you are and why.

All Awareness

Finally, in stage five, you begin to realize that you are more than a simple being. There are more people, things, and spirits in this realm than we have fingers and toes. Entities of all shapes and sizes exist beside us - some real, and some just creations of our minds. We are each more than the sum of our parts - and we aren't alone. This has nothing to do with a belief system. Even scientists have accepted that there are things we can't explain. Accepting possibilities is a prominent feature in this stage. If you can accept the unreal, that there might be something unknown - you're in stage five.

It's during this stage that we begin to accept the darkness within us. You begin to understand that there are some parts of you that you can't change and that you don't want to explore. You'll find inhuman traits inside you that you wish you didn't have, your thoughts about yourself and your flaws become more complex, and you realize our version of right and wrong is sublimely simplified.

By coming to terms with your dark side, you also begin to see the dark and light in others. You develop the ability to understand and predict intentions.

PART 3

Lucid Dreaming Guide

If you have been reading along on your Kindle, iPad, or online source, now is the time to change over to the Audio Guide. If you don't have access to one, ensure that you set your alarms at the intervals mentioned.

Dr. Stephen LaBerge invented a technique called mnemonic induction, MILD, to evoke lucid dreams on demand (Turner, n.d.). It's a very effective method and ideal for beginners.

This guide will now take you through the MILD method. This method will improve your self-awareness and make it easier to become lucid while dreaming. It will also help you remember your goals in a dream and follow through on them.

His technique works by planting a cue in your mind to help recall your intentions within the dream.

Before you can practice mnemonic induction, you must be able to recall a few past dreams. Keeping a dream journal can help you recall the vividness of your dreams, the sequences of events, and your feelings.

Next, throughout the day, you must regularly perform reality checks. A reality check involves asking yourself if you are awake or dreaming. Don't answer the question mentally, answer it physically. Perform a movement that allows you to identify your state of mind. For example, if you are awake, you can walk up to a door and open it; but, if you are dreaming, you'll most likely fly through the door.

If you become experienced in establishing reality checks, it becomes easier to trigger a moment of introspection while asleep.

Now that you have practiced your reality checks, take the MILD method a step further. As you settle into bed for the night, state your intention aloud or internally:

- When I dream, I will know I am dreaming.

- The next scene I experience will be a dream.

- I will have a lucid dream.

- I am dreaming right now.

These affirmations will prepare your mind for what needs to happen.

As you are drifting off to sleep, visualize your dream before you enter it, and know exactly where you are going. Then, the second you start dreaming, do a reality check. If you start to fly, or objects begin to levitate, you will know you are dreaming.

The following guide will help you prepare for bed. It will show you a variety of physical and mental strategies that can be used to help you wind down. This section will also include a few nighttime recipes that will stir your consciousness while you sleep, and a few affirmations and sleeping plans to prepare you for the adventures to come.

You will then be led through two guided meditations. The first will occur about thirty minutes before you enter the first stage of sleep, while the second will occur after the first alarm goes off. It is a good idea to set the first alarm 90 minutes before you are supposed to wake up. If you need to wake up at 7:00, set the alarm to 5:30. You should set a second alarm for when you wish to wake up for the day and finish your lucid dreaming practice.

When you wake up, return to the second section of the guide, where you'll be led through a few more lucid dreaming affirmations. Here, you will have the chance to remind yourself where you want to go and what you want to do. Another meditation guide will help you fall back asleep.

Your final alarm will go off and wake you for the day.

CHAPTER 7

Bed-Time Preparations

Planning Where You Want To Go

Think about where you want to go.

- What does the place look like?

- Is it day or night?

- Is the air warm or cold?

- What kind of sounds can you hear as you walk through?

- Are there animals around?

- Or other people?

- Who are those people?

- What are they wearing?

- Who are they to you?

- Do they make you happy?

- Do they excite you?

- What are you doing there?

- Are you simply walking about and enjoying the view?

- Do you have another purpose?

- Does your purpose frighten or excite you?

- How do you plan on achieving this purpose?

- Are you going to run somewhere?

- Are you going to learn a new skill?

- Do you have to memorize something?

- Do you have to create something new?

Lastly:

- How do you see your dream ending?

- Were you successful in fulfilling your purpose?

- If you were, how so?

- What did you do that made things end well?

- Would you do anything differently?

Try to memorize some of these answers, or write them down and reread them before you fall asleep. These will be the elements to look out for in your dream.

Letting Go of Bad Experiences

Lucid dreaming can sometimes lead to some difficult-to-explain experiences. In the lucid dream where I saw my dearly departed grandmother, I had the strange experience of feeling my mind leave my body. That alone was perplexing. Along with that, I had decided to travel down the tunnels of a mirror and had to witness the distortion of my face repeatedly. When I finally plummeted onto a field of dandelions and sunflowers, I could feel the fear grow inside of me and forced myself awake, too afraid to practice further.

Experiences like these are common, especially among beginners and individuals with high stress levels. If you have experienced nightmarish lucidity within a dream, or happen to experience one while using this guide, remove yourself from the dream, take time to recover, and try again when you are ready.

Remember, your dreams are just a scattering of images and ideas. They have no meaning unless you assign them meaning. You don't need to spend long hours analyzing nightmares that cause you grief and misery. You can experience other dreams that will reveal the same things far more pleasantly.

Once you have recovered, put the dream behind you and start anew.

Valerian Root Tea Recipe

One of my favorite teas is valerian root. Valerian root is a popular herbal tea that not only boosts dream recall but has also been said to brighten the colors of one's dreams. Its bitter taste and grassy odor will immerse you into a forest landscape within seconds.

Valerian root also has muscle relaxant properties which will help relieve any tension you might still feel after a long day. Half a mug is more than enough.

Wait? Half a mug?

Well, if you're the kind of coffee drinker I am, your mug is about the size of your kettle – so half a mug of tea is more than enough. Too much water before bed can overstimulate your hypothalamus and make it impossible for your brain to switch off.

Remember, you only need to keep the prefrontal cortex awake.

Though I love bitter tastes, my partner prefers the sweeter things in life. Two teaspoons of honey and a cinnamon stick are the additions he swears by. You can choose to try the same if the tea is too bitter for you.

Relaxation Exercise

We're going to turn it down now. Find a comfortable space on the floor in your room. If the space doesn't feel big enough, find one in the lounge. If you'd prefer to use the bathroom floor, lay a towel down for warmth.

Physical

Lie on your back, keeping your knees bent and your feet

positioned naturally in front of your buttocks. Lay your hands on your stomach and just breathe. Try to keep your eyes open. You may need to switch off the light before continuing.

Are you comfortable?

You should not be feeling any tension in your body in this position. If you are, change it up. Make sure you are comfortable.

Just breathe. Let the thoughts and worries of the day enter your mind and slip back out. Don't force yourself not to think about them. They are crucial because they are important to you. You'll deal with them later.

Keep breathing.

Think of one thing today that made you angry.

Have you got it?

Now, I want you to replace that thought with one thing from the day that made you proud of yourself. Let that pride slip into the place of your anger. Smile, even if you don't want to.

Now, get up onto your knees. Place your hands on the floor; you should feel like a cat in this position. Take in a deep breath. As you do, arch your back upwards. Let the tension from the day fill your shoulders and your neck. Breathe out, and as you do, let your back fall naturally back to its original position.

Stay like this for a minute and breathe gently. You should repeat this exercise a few times until the tension in your shoulders goes away.

I want you to breathe in and arch your back, hold your position for a few seconds, and then release. You should let your posture fall back to normal.

That was very good.

Take a few more moments to breathe before you try this again.

Breathe in and arch your back, hold, and release.

Continue and repeat this exercise at your own pace.

Poem of Strength

Here is a poem to remind you of how inspirational you are. Read this aloud or in your head:

You are special because you are alive,

you may not think yourself strong but you are.

You are still here, your roots built to just thrive

as you grow above the thorns on hard tar.

You came to stand where it wasn't possible.

Why cry over your dried and spoiled leaves?

Didn't you know that dead stems are more beautiful

in summer when they sprout their flowers plenty?

You are glorious, lovely, and so kind.

Any who cannot see so are out of their mind.

Psychological

How do you feel?

A little more relaxed, I hope.

I want you to stand up now - slowly, there is no rush - and slowly move about your house, turning off any light that may have been left on. If you happen to see laundry on the floor, or dishes in the sink, take a breath and let them be. You are more important now.

Once the house is quiet and locked up for the night, settle in your bed and set your first and second alarms.

In your mind, I want you to visualize a circle being drawn. Picture the edges and how they morph into one another. Start small and gradually begin to draw larger and larger circles.

I want you to imagine that you are that circle. You are whole, even if it doesn't always feel that way. You are complete, even if you don't think you have everything you need right now. You, alone, are the fullness of what you are meant to be. You don't need any other edges or beings or shapes to form your circle. You are enough.

Like any circle, you need to cycle through a series of sleep stages so you can heal and deal with another day.

Affirmation for Relaxation

Say this affirmation aloud or in your head to help you relax:

I am whole. I am complete. I don't always feel it and I don't always recognize it, but I am.

I am my own person. I make my own decisions and I am grounded by the things I need to help me.

No one else can take my importance away. No child, partner, career, or friend is worth any damage to my value.

I am important.

Right now, I am the most important.

I deserve to rest. I deserve to feel the wholeness of my body and my mind. I deserve to feel myself being alive.

I need to sleep. This is for me.

Chapter 8

Sleep Affirmations

I have found a selection of affirmations for varying purposes. Select the ones most compatible with you and your goals, and feel free to repeat them out loud or in your head.

Alleviating Nightmares

Tonight, I will not be plagued by fear or sadness. I will only feel hope and wonder as I encounter and interact with my dreams. There is no monster in my head large enough to toy with my feelings tonight. I am in control of my emotions. I am in control of what I see. I am in control of what I know. If what I encounter makes me uncomfortable, I will change it. I am the master of my dreams. I am in control of my own peace. I am in charge of the rest I receive. No pain, stress, or fear will touch me tonight.

Good, Deep Sleep

I have worked as hard as I can. I have sweated all the energy from my body. I have cooked all the meals I can, and I have planned as far as planning will take me. I am deserving of deep and restful sleep. Tonight, nothing will wake me. Nothing will frighten me, and nothing will disturb my thoughts. I am here, I am present, and I am ready to sleep. I will close my eyes and when I open them again in the morning, I will feel refreshed and healed. My body will not flutter, and my mind will not tolerate anything beyond my need for sleep. I will rest deeply and safely and better than I ever have before.

Sweet Dreams

I have seen and experienced many stressful things today. I will not encounter the same fate in my dreams. When I close my eyes and fall into a slumber, I will be greeted by the sweetest and kindest of faces. I will laugh and love as I have never done before. I will chase after my favorite adventures and wander into my most loved lands. I will encounter stories of wonder, peace, and hope. Tonight, my dreams will be sweet and bring me a day's worth of happiness when I wake up. I will feel loved and appreciated in my sleep. I will know that I am valued, and I will have nothing to worry about. No harm or stress will touch me while I dream tonight. I am worthy of hopeful thinking. I am deserving of the sweetest of thoughts. I will experience joy in my dreams tonight.

Lucid Dreaming

Do you remember the preparations you did before bed? Do you remember where you wanted to go? Now is the time to think about that place and your answers to the questions asked. I want you to say this affirmation aloud or in your head.

Tonight, I will go exactly where I want. The place will be exactly as I imagined. I will feel how I dreamt I would feel. There will be no discrepancies. I will see the things I want to see. I will fulfill my purpose. I will be successful in my endeavors. I will uncover all the truths I wish to uncover, and I will wake up remembering my adventure with refreshed and healed eyes.

CHAPTER 9

Guided Sleep Meditations and Alarms

The First Guided Sleep Meditation

By now, your brain should be settling into snooze mode. Follow this open sleep meditation guide to help you set your intentions.

Close your eyes. Don't be afraid, you are not alone.

Breathe in deeply and feel your body sinking into the bed, falling deeper into your blankets.

Give your sheets a little rub. Acknowledge where you are. Trust that your room looks the same as when you last saw it. The bed sheets are the same color, the floor feels the same, and your pictures are in the same place you put them. Keep rubbing your sheets, but don't open your eyes. You're not crazy; you know what your home looks like. Trust your mind. Trust your body as it tells you it is feeling sleepy.

Breathe in and breathe out.

Let your body sink deeper into the blankets.

Acknowledge the weight of the sheets on your feet. Acknowledge the heaviness of the blankets on your chest.

Breathe in and breathe out.

Let those last little thoughts slip from your mind. They don't matter now. You matter. You are tired. You are deserving of peace. You are allowed to let go of reality. I am here - I will hold onto it for you until you wake up.

Breathe in.

Let your shoulders fall back into the bed with your spine.

Breathe in.

Let your chest fall back with your shoulders.

There is no right or wrong way to sleep.

Let go of the sheet you have been rubbing.

It will still be there in the morning.

You will still be here in the morning.

You want to be here in the morning.

You want to share with your loved ones the strange and wonderful dream you had.

Have that dream now.

Breathe in and out.

See the floors of the place you travel to. See the road as it curves. Feel the wind in your hair and the sun on your skin.

There is nowhere else you need to be.

Sleep.

Breathe in and breathe out.

Let your head slip into the pillow. You don't need to hold it up anymore. Let your lips part if they want to. You don't need to keep your mouth closed now. Tell your ears to hear what they will - nothing is going to disturb you on your journey into the land of dreams.

Poem For Sleep

Here is a poem to help you fall asleep easier. You can say it aloud or in your head.

Shall I switch off your sun, my darling shell?

Leave that very switch under your pillow?

Eyes need not see streams of light while sleep swells

effortlessly under sheets laid over

your worn toes, sleepy arms, and tired shoulders.

Sounds come and stars shine, yet you are not stirred

Lies your mind now, someplace sweeter than this?

Enchanted by flirting winds and bright birds

Easing over wondrous ocean waves

Playing in the sun of a brand new day.

Need I ask where you go, my darling shell?

Or should I not wake you from your dream well?

Worry not, I'll ask you in the morrow.

Sleep, sleep now.

Shall I meet you there, my sweet sleeping shell?

Waking—The First Alarm

Do you still remember where you want to go and what you want to achieve?

Affirmations For Taking Control

Feel free to repeat this affirmation in your head or out loud.

Now, I will travel to the place I want to go.

I see it in my mind. I know how the land curves against the sky. I recognize the birds as they sing. I know this place. I know how I got here. I know the roads to take and the streams to cross. I know the houses and people, the animals, and the smells. I know this place. I want to be in this place. I will go to this place now and do what I have been longing to do. Nothing will stop me. No dream is more important than this one. This is the place I want to be and so I will find myself there.

The Second Guided Sleep Meditation

You are traveling to the place you want to be. You are calm. You have traveled this route many times before. You have studied the landscape and the people. You know how to get there and are confident in that. On the horizon, you can see a landmark, bright and bold, signaling you have arrived. You find yourself amidst the landscape you know so well. The weather is how you have always known it to be. You are at peace here. There is nothing that can disturb you in this place. You have a purpose here. You have a duty. Take a step forward and into that purpose now.

Don't look back. Let your mind open. Let go. Sleep now.

The Second Alarm

It is a new day, and I want you to take a breath and let the morning air flood your body. I want you to remind yourself of your fingers and toes. Move them and wriggle them beneath your covers.

Breathe in deep and breathe out, and as you do, rub your sheets between your fingers.

Nothing has moved. Nothing has changed. You are a little more rested than you were before.

Now, you can conquer a new day and do amazing things.

You may or may not have experienced exactly what you were hoping to experience. Remember that the study of dreams and lucid dreaming is still new in the science community. When you are ready, try again.

Very few people can lucid dream naturally. Whether or not this ability is connected to your ancestral evolutionary development, no one knows. However, we can presume that the ability started with the growth of the prefrontal cortex in Homo sapiens.

The point is - don't be disheartened if guided meditation didn't work out the first time around. Lick your wounds, take time to analyze what you learned about yourself, and try again when you feel ready.

The benefits of learning such a skill are numerous. Don't let yourself lose out because of a few failed attempts. You can do this. You already have the knowledge and the understanding to accomplish this. All you need is time and practice.

Don't give up.

Journal Entries

Now is the time to write down any experiences you may have encountered, even if it was something as small as hearing the ocean before you dozed off.

If you can't remember your dreams, that is okay. Write down what you do remember, even if it is something that happened before you switched off the lights. When you read through your journal entries later, you may recall a thought or a scene that you experienced.

Dream journaling is a great way to practice remembering your dreams.

Once you have achieved that, you can analyze and use them.

Affirmations for the Day

I have found a selection of waking affirmations to help you set your intentions for the day. Select the ones that fit you and your goals and feel free to say them out loud or in your head.

Taking Control Throughout Your Day

I am in control of my feelings, thoughts, and actions. I know what is best for me and my body. I am not afraid to voice my ideas and concerns. I am in charge of my needs and how they are met. I am responsible for my own needs, wants, and thoughts. I am in control of my time. I am the only one who knows how to manage it best. I am confident in who I am and, today, I am going to take this world by storm.

Removing Stress and Anxiety

I am in control of my feelings. I sense and acknowledge my stress and anxiety. I acknowledge all the things I must do today. I know what works for me and I'll stick to it. If I don't know how to approach a task or a setting, I'll give myself time to consider it. Life is not so fast that I can't be afforded one minute to think before I act. I am deserving of that one minute. Everyone else can wait that one minute.

I will not be rushed today. I will not let my anxiety control me today. There is nothing so important that I have to relinquish my control. I am important. I am more important than any task, event, or object. I breathe and therefore deserve the same peace I try to give others. I am in control today - not anyone or anything else, and certainly not a bout of sad, unwanted anxiety.

Remembering

I am in control of my thoughts today. I acknowledge that I am not a robot. I acknowledge that there will be times when I will forget things. I will do my best not to. I have planned things out strategically. I will move slowly and cautiously. I will trust my decisions because I know I have spent the time making them. I will remember the things that are important today. I will remember the things that matter to me. Should I forget something, I will not beat myself to a pulp about it. I am doing my best and no one can ask more of me.

I have done everything in my power to remember the things I need to. I have made a list. I have memorized the list. I have talked to people about the list and placed the list in a place I look at often. I will do my best and take peace from that. I will not strive for perfection. Me, my mistakes, and my forgetfulness are perfect enough. I am remarkable for trying to remember everything that I have to do today.

Peace and Happiness

Today, I am going to have a great day. I am not going to let anything bring me down. I am a strong and wonderful person. I acknowledge my flaws. I accept that I am going to make mistakes. I know that, at some point, I may make someone's life a little harder. That is okay. I choose to understand myself, my potential mistakes, my flaws, and my issues. I am understanding because I know that my worth, kindness, creativity, and talent make up for the moments when I do not shine at my brightest. I am doing my best. I choose to be kind today. I choose to be happy today. I choose to be at peace with my decisions and mistakes today. Nothing and no one is going to make me feel otherwise.

PART 4

Understanding Your Subconscious

From the types of dreams you have to the figures within them, your mind is a complex organ that takes some getting used to. Knowing the reasons why you might be having certain dreams can help you understand your deepest needs and desires. When we are awake, our minds are locked. When we sleep, however, we are open to countless opportunities and ideas. Allow your dreams to guide you to your desires and what you need to do to get it.

Use the following chapters to help you understand your mind better and remember that you are the only person with the whole truth. Don't be afraid to look within and find the answers you need. They might be different from the ones offered here. Be brave - you've come so far already. Now, all you need is a pen and paper to jot down your ideas.

Lucid dreaming will give you a chance to live the life you always wanted. It gives you the chance to meet your greatest heroes, go places you've only dreamed of going, fly, break away from toxic relationships, and begin new ones. When you live, you gain experience, and access something that only comes with time - wisdom. The more you live and the more spontaneous you are, the more you learn. So, get out there in your sleep and live! Fly and fall from the skies. Ride horses backward and learn why you shouldn't put brandy in your car's gas tank. Ask complicated questions about your future, past, your present. Learn everything you can about yourself.

While you're living your best life, take the time to heal yourself. Heal those parts you think are broken and give yourself a chance to sparkle again. Realize your fears and get rid of them. Understand why you are the way you are by looking into your past. You can even change who you are by going back into your memories and changing what you believe happened. Anything is possible. You can even heal your heart so you can love again. You can go for intense foot massages so that you can feel balanced. Exercise in your dreams and lose weight so that you can feel good and healthy again. You will be amazed at the results.

Take your dream a step further and plan your success for your waking life. Finally, take those fantasies and make them a reality in the present. You can do this by making a list of how you want to live your life. At bedtime, refer to this list so that you can ask your subconscious how you can achieve your goals and make the most of your life.

You deserve to live the life you envision. You deserve to have a wine cabinet, a nice kitchen, and that beautiful garden. You deserve to win a triathlon and go to Wimbledon. You can do anything you want in this life - you already know this. Now, let your dreams be your guide.

CHAPTER 10

Looking at Your Dreams

Identifying Types of Dreams, Themes, and Feelings

Standard Dreams

Standard dreams are the most common type of dreams and usually consist of symbols and imagery with little significance. In a standard dream, there are no significant bodily changes, challenging emotions, or overly dramatic scenes. Your heart rate and breathing remain relatively normal. After experiencing a standard dream, most people don't try to find the meaning behind it, because there is little that needs to be probed further.

Having a standard dream is a great starting point for dream analysis, as these dreams don't elicit emotional stress. You shouldn't expect to unpack your worst fears through a standard dream.

One night, while on a camping trip with a group of friends, I dreamt that I was at a great party:

Everyone was having a blast and drinking champagne. The women were twirling around in 18th-century dresses, and the men bowed before them in an attempt to sweep them off their feet. All was well, until a group of ninjas attacked the party. What they didn't know was that all the guests were hand-to-hand combat experts. With bravery and honor, the group managed to chase off the ninjas.

When morning came, I remember one of my friends asking what made me laugh so loudly in my sleep.

The way one feels during a dream and when they wake up is pivotal in recognizing what kind of dream they experienced and its meaning. If I had been terrified in my dream and woken up in cold sweat, I would have called it a nightmare. I was happy in my dream, happy when I woke, and today I remember my dream fondly. Therefore, this is a standard dream and should be analyzed as such.

Let's look at some of the themes in the dream: positivity, violence, grandeur, entertainment, historical, and surrealism. If we put these themes into context, they start to make a bit more sense. A camping trip with friends is a positive and entertaining experience. The themes of grandeur and historical clothing could represent the character traits of my very feminine and excitable friends.

But, what about the violence?

Young girls argue (if you didn't know) a lot. As an adult, it can be quite entertaining to watch young girls in a group successfully diffuse one argument, only to move on to another - and then successfully diffuse that. I remember, as a child, rambling into multiple arguments with my friends, but still managing to find my way out without crumbling under the pressure. I remember always testing what buttons were worth pressing, only to scamper away as quickly as possible so I wouldn't get called out as a troublemaker. Young boys do this too, but I always thought they weren't as quick to get out of trouble as girls. Of course, that's not to be said for all of them.

My point is, if you look at how young girls interact, the vision of fighting ninjas in a fun and spontaneous way makes sense. Everything in my dream was merely a recap of what I was experiencing in my waking life.

We could also look into the meaning of the symbols in the dream to get a more accurate idea of what I was experiencing at the time. Ninjas and 18th-century parties in dreams represent passive-aggressive behavior and competition, respectively.

Suddenly, my crazy dream started to sound more like the standard dream of a young girl who's been hanging out a bit with her friends.

I analyzed this dream when I was in my thirties. But imagine who I would have been and how I would have interacted with my friends if I'd known what my dream meant back then. I might have stopped fumbling with ideas of competitiveness at an earlier age. I might have been able to prevent the arguments I had with friends and maintained more female friendships.

Imagine how every kid would be like if they could develop empathy and engage in introspection at an earlier age. All they need to do is analyze their dreams.

Sex Dreams

Have you ever woken up in the middle of the night feeling sexy, hot, and bothered? Have your dreams ever resulted in late-night orgasms? Sex dreams and their meanings aren't always literal. Although they might be a portrayal of your desire for sex and intimacy, they are often apparitions of our desires, worries, and anxieties.

A dream involving oral sex could reveal your desire for more communication in your waking life, or it could be the result of a recent experience involving a good conversation.

I frequently experience sexual dreams. They first started when I comfortably settled with my partner. I was so happy, and I couldn't understand why my dreams would constantly involve sex with other men. Instead of allowing myself to feel guilty about these dreams, I looked into why I liked those men. I liked how they dressed, their scent, and how they asked me how I was doing. It seemed to me that any affection I had for them was connected to things, traits, or behaviors my partner wasn't providing. So, I challenged myself to do something about it.

What if I asked my partner to do these things for me? Would that change anything?

It worked. I asked my partner to dress nicely for our dates, for us to talk about our days and our feelings, for us to take long showers together, and blanket one another in perfumes. It worked. The dreams and feelings attached to those dreams went away.

On one occasion, I dreamt I was being held rather provocatively by my boss. I asked my partner to take more control of our relationship, plan dates, and cook dinners - which he did - and the dreams stopped.

My dreams helped me analyze my relationship and improve it. I don't feel guilty for having those dreams.

Why should I feel guilty about wanting more?

I don't want to cheat on my partner. That's not what those dreams meant for me. My dreams were telling me what I desired to stay in the relationship. Once I knew what these things were, I felt comfortable exploring these needs with my partner, ensuring we both got what we wanted so we could have a healthy and happy partnership.

There are people in relationships who are itching to get out, and you might be one of them. My advice is to let your subconscious be your guide. If you want an affair, speak to your partner. Maybe they need a break as much as you. Perhaps there is a deeper meaning in your need to escape your relationship. Your subconscious mind may be trying to tell you your partner isn't right for you.

That's where the "me" versus "you" concept comes in. Only you can know what your dreams are trying to tell you. I could be way off the mark here. You could be more like me or have a different idea of what's going on. There are no rules when it comes to dream analysis - there is only you and your truth. You know that truth better than anyone.

What about sex dreams when you're not in a relationship?

It's the same - penetrative sex, oral sex, and fondling all represent the desire to have something you don't currently have. A sex dream with a family member, although it can leave you astoundingly uncomfortable, might represent your desire to communicate more with that person. A sex dream with a stranger might represent your desire for spontaneity, excitement, or pleasure. After having a sex dream, try doing something you enjoy, like going for a walk or baking. Maybe invite friends over for a night of drinking or go out dancing. A sex dream doesn't always mean you need sex, but it does mean you need something. Reach out in your dream and ask. The answer might surprise you - or it might not.

Lucid Dreams

If you haven't quite understood what lucid dreaming is, that's okay. It took scientists thousands of years to come to grips with it, and they couldn't fully understand it without the help of cats. So, grab a companion and see if you can figure this out together.

Recurring Dreams

Some people will experience the same dream, repeatedly, for years.

I had one particularly alarming nightmare while I was growing up:

I was a knight dressed in medieval uniform atop a castle tower. I felt a fear stirring in my body - a warning that something was about to happen.

The more I had this dream, the more I remembered where I had to go and what my purpose in it was. The first time I had it, I didn't know anything.

I followed my senses toward a turret. There, I entered a room that was so dark that I couldn't see anything. Suddenly, I was attacked by the ghost of another knight. In a frightful frenzy, I battled this unseen knight, whose sword kept sweeping in and out of existence.

Every night, for much of my youth, I woke up in a sweaty panic.

Every time I had that dream, it extended slightly. As I got older, I became used to the scenes and how the dream played out. I started to remember where the ghost would move and how it would react. It was like playing a video game. Eventually, you know exactly when to accelerate and when to hold back because the game is always the same. How quickly you react to certain throws - which may come with practice or intuition - is what helps you win in the end.

The last time I had this dream - I think I was about 18 - I

defeated the ghost and I never had the dream again.

Why did this dream occur so often? Why did it keep extending? Why couldn't I defeat the ghost at age 14? Why did it only happen when I was 18?

Let's analyze my dream to try and find these answers.

The themes in my complex nightmare are violence, death, ghosts, and knights.

I researched these symbols, and here is what I found: Violence in dreams symbolizes guilt. In my case, because I was being abused, the guilt was toward myself.

What did I feel guilty about?

Let's include the theme of death as we further explore my guilt. Death represents change. It's common for a young child to have dreams involving death. Being so young means that children are the most prone to changes and dreams of death. I was likely feeling guilty about changing. There is always a part of us that wants to accept and love who we are. In my case, I wanted to love myself, but I also wanted to change and become a person who could experience life without all the challenges. I didn't want the emotional baggage that poverty brought. I didn't want the trauma from all the fighting that surrounded me. Yet, I also did, because that was my life and who I was. I felt guilty for wanting to change, and for changing.

A ghost symbolizes the fear of death or change. That is exactly what I just expressed. As a child, I was fearful and anxious about the changes I was experiencing.

A knight represents security, while the sword symbolizes bravery. Why was I fighting security, and why was bravery slipping away from me?

Throughout my childhood, I lived in less than ideal circumstances. My family didn't have mountains of security, love, and finances to bestow upon me. All they could do was love me as much as they were able to. When offered more, I naturally wanted to take that security; but how could I when my family was on the other side of that fence? I didn't want to leave them there. So, the need for security and a normal life beat me over and over. I couldn't find myself brave enough to say, "Enough! This is what I want and wherever I am, I will always love you."

When I turned 18 and finally found the courage to break away from the ongoing poverty, that was the moment I was finally able to defeat the ghost, accept that I was different, and lead myself toward a path of security, refuge, and better finances.

This dream was my mind's way of coping with the idea that I wanted more than what my family could offer.

Visitation Dreams

This is a special category and probably one of the biggest reasons why dreaming is so often linked with the esoteric. When someone you care about passes away, the brain processes massive amounts of information, feelings, hormones, and chemicals – intrinsic and extrinsic. Your amygdala, which controls your memories and your emotions, works overtime, showering you with memories of your loved ones and causing you to break down in a flood of tears at the most inopportune of times. Your mind tries to forgive you for these outbursts, but it's so busy processing your need to sleep, eat, drink, and still get to work on time that you're often left feeling guilty.

In addition, the psychological trauma caused by grief can manifest physically and cause hair loss, rashes, and drops in the immune system, leading to illness. Your mind fumbles between finding excuses and blaming yourself for your downfall.

It's no wonder your mind pines for relief at night after the day's suffering.

A visitation dream involves seeing or hearing a deceased loved one.

I'm sure individuals involved in esotericism or spiritualism will provide you with a wealth of meaning behind seeing your departed loved one at nighttime. From a scientific standpoint, this is your body's way of healing.

What if that loved one passed on months or even years ago? Why would they visit now?

Your brain is constantly processing information. That one word you heard your mom say in Spanish over the phone when you were a kid, is still being processed.

Ever wonder how babies can suddenly go from saying one- or two-word fragments to speaking whole sentences? It's because their brains are always processing the information input over time.

So you see, it's not unfathomable that, months after a departure, you might find yourself still thinking about the person. Losing someone is especially hard; it's one of the most difficult things a person can go through. The mind can't possibly process everything it needs to while you are grieving. When you finally stop grieving, your mind will revisit that need to say goodbye and give you that chance.

When I was in my twenties, my grandmother passed away rather unexpectedly. Her passing was traumatic for the whole family, and so I couldn't deal with the pain that it caused until years after. During one Sunday afternoon nap, I found myself in a field of golden chrysanthemums, her favorite flower.

There she was, walking happily and undisturbed in the meadow.

This was one of the first dreams I had after returning from my retreat. I told you about it very briefly in "Part 1."

Let's take the chance, now, to analyze this dream further.

The themes in this dream were: flowers, light, and visitation.

Flowers in a dream represent happiness and joy, and sunlight represents victory and prosperity: to live on. These meanings, combined with the vision of my gran walking happily in a meadow, show that my mind knew her soul was at peace. It was through lucid dreaming that my subconscious was able to relay this information to my waking mind so that I could truly come to terms with her passing.

But not all dreams are as simple and believable. As with anything in science, there will be inexplicable cases.

I'll give an example. I had a friend in college who told me about a dream she had experienced the previous night. She explained how she had awoken to a fiery, ash-stricken face staring at her.

The face hadn't frightened her, but after looking at it from a few angles, she decided to double-check that she wasn't going crazy and that the face was there. She turned on the light switch, looked again, and the face was gone.

Later, in the afternoon, it was announced that a student had died in a fire in one of the on-campus residences.

Did she see the face of the student who had passed away?

Fire in a dream represents hidden understanding and meaning. A burnt face in a dream represents a connection between the spiritual and living worlds. Whether she saw the face of the student who passed, or her dream was revealing her ability to speak to those who have passed over, only she can answer.

Another theory could be that, subconsciously, she could hear the flames flickering in the night and her brain put two and two together and created a visual.

Her dream could also have been a coincidence.

What she thinks is what matters most. I know she believes the dream was a coincidence, one that made her look at life with a little more meaning.

"We never know how much time we have. If he was a ghost, he

gave me a gift. If he wasn't, I think my brain needs a holiday."

She was studying engineering - she could have been going crazy.

Psychic Dreams

This type of dream has amassed numerous spiritual explanations. For centuries, people have claimed that their dreams are psychic visions, images of the future. Nostradamus is a strong lead character in this.

There is no proof that Nostradamus dreamt his predictions, only that he calculated the possibility of similar events happening. For example, there is no mention of Adolf Hitler or COVID in his works. Rather, Nostradamus predicted that a man of German descent would bring about a great war. Similarly, he predicted a great pandemic would cause socialization to stand still.

Scientists from around the world are still trying to prove which war and pandemic he was referring to, along with an array of other events he predicted. Nonetheless, he is a fascinating topic of discussion, and you'll find many works exploring the plausibility of his visions.

In the same capacity, scientists aren't sure if certain dreams are psychic visions or your brain's way of processing possible outcomes.

Athletes do this when they train with performance psychologists. Using visual imagery techniques and lucid dreaming activities, athletes will dream their game plans, practice their run-offs, and run through various situations.

Suddenly, the opponent dives on top of you, and you roll out quickly, ducking your head on your shoulder. You pass the ball sideways to your teammate, who manages to make a beeline for the goal post. He kicks. He scores. The game is over, with your team winning 3 to 1.

The next day comes. You get tackled, but you manage to get out and toss the ball to your teammate, who scores, and it all seems oddly familiar.

Most athletes have done this - they've processed their reactions to certain events thousands of times, consciously and subconsciously.

I had a friend who swore that they could predict the future after they experienced a dream that turned into reality.

They dreamt that their dog had fallen into the swimming pool. In the dream, they ran toward their pet and scooped them out of the water.

The next day, it happened.

Maybe they could predict the future or maybe they had noticed that the pool gate had been left open. The dream was their subconscious mind trying to remind them to close it.

Dogs in dreams symbolize protection. Falling into pools represents the anxieties and fears experienced in childhood. It's possible my friend felt as though their current form of protection wasn't substantial and was compelled to step in and become the hero. It's common for children to realize that their parents aren't superheroes. When this happens, most kids will begin to take life into their own hands. It's a good thing because it means they are becoming more independent. Maybe this is what my friend was going through, and the incident that occurred the next day was just proof of what they already knew - that he could provide for and protect his family.

At the end of the day, no one else can tell you what your dreams mean.

Daydreams

Daydreams are visual or audible scenes that play out in your head during the day while you are awake. Children are some of the best daydreamers I have ever met. Whether you're explaining algebra or how to fold laundry, they will find a way to daydream and ignore everything you are saying - even when they are looking right at you.

In most cases, daydreams are simply your imagination playing around to entertain you. They're easy to remember and fun to engage with.

Daydreams can also be a way to alleviate stress, be creative, or explore conversations and events in a socially acceptable way.

It's not right to hit your sibling over the head with a book when they annoy you, but you can daydream about it.

If you find yourself struggling to remember your dreams, try engaging with a daydream. It's as simple as imagining yourself in a scenario and then reacting in that scenario.

Here's something to help start you off:

You're walking in the jungle when you see a tiger. What happens?

If you're someone who struggles to remember dreams, you might say something like, "Well, I get eaten and that's the end of it" or "Why am I in a jungle? I don't even like being outside."

Remember that there is no right or wrong answer. Both answers are correct and reveal a lot about who you are. In practicing lucid dreaming though, it's important to always think about what happens next.

For example:

I was walking in the jungle. I saw a tiger.

Of course, I was afraid, and so I ran away. The tiger ran after me. I approached a stream and dived in, allowing the water to take me far away from the threat of being eaten.

Moving streams lead to waterfalls, though, and so...

Try to finish the rest for yourself. Don't think too much about it. Just use whatever comes to mind.

Nightmares

I am sure you have been itching to learn more about the darker side of sleeping.

Let's be very clear here - there is a big difference between a nightmare and a bad dream. Night terrors, nightmares, and sleep paralysis all contain traits that make them different.

A bad dream is simply a standard dream that doesn't cause any, or many, bodily changes and, while it may not be a good start to your morning, most people forget their bad dreams by lunchtime.

A nightmare is very different because during the dream, the individual's heart will race, their breathing will quicken, and their amygdala will light up as fear takes over their body. When they wake up, they become immediately alert and may still be frightened. As their day continues, they may still feel agitated by the content of the dream, which they may or may not remember.

A nightmare is frightening. I'll give an example of one, maybe adding some unwanted humor to the situation.

If I told you I had a nightmare that my teddy bear came to life, you might snort and ask, "Isn't that every kid's fantasy?"

But, to say this would be disregarding the term "nightmare" and the effects of having one. It is not what happens in a nightmare that makes it scary; it's the illogical fear that arises.

Remember that, when it comes to analyzing dreams, focusing on the type of dream is only a part of the process.

Let's look at the themes that may be present in a nightmare where a teddy bear comes to life.

These might include body dysmorphia, unnatural moving of

objects, unrecognizable sounds, and unpredicted events.

Now, a larger and more detailed picture is starting to come together. Perhaps the nightmare is the brain's way of processing that it doesn't feel comfortable in its own body.

This could be for a variety of reasons. Perhaps the individual has recently lost a limb. The nightmare could also signify the concerns of an anxious planner.

Imagine a mother planning a school trip for fifty kids. What happens if one of those kids decides to do their own thing, wanders off, and then doesn't come back?

These are all very real fears that might not be immediately apparent.

What if you have a similar nightmare, but you can't help laughing it off and thinking, "Oh, brain, what have you gone and thought about now?" It's remarkable that you can shake off a fright like that.

Many other people can't do that and, often, where there is one nightmare, there are more.

Night Terrors

People who suffer from frequent nightmares sometimes

confuse their painful sleep with night terrors. Night terrors are a scary phenomenon to witness, often more so than experiencing them. Many people who suffer from night terrors don't remember what happened.

Do you remember that, during sleep, the motor neurons in your brain become inhibited to stop you from acting out your dreams? With sleepwalkers, this isn't always the case.

Night terrors are similar. The individual won't get up or walk around, but they will enact their dreams as they lay in bed, often thrashing and kicking at the sheets. In some cases, the dreamer can sit up and have a conversation with their attacker.

People from across the world talk, laugh, and cry in their sleep every day. I've even experienced moments when a friend will be sleeping and talking, I'll ask them a question, and they'll respond with a most humorous and ludicrous response. No one is possessed and no one is in danger - except for the dreamer within their minds.

Accounts of night terrors include battling monsters, outrunning attackers, and even drowning.

The reasons behind these dreams and themes are numerous. A night terror involving drowning could mean the individual is under a lot of pressure or feels like they can't cope. A dream involving outrunning attackers may signal that the dreamer feels as though they are keeping too many secrets or that everyone hates them. The meaning of the dream may differ depending on one's race, ethnicity, or even gender.

I'll say it again - dreams can only be truly analyzed by the dreamer.

Sleep Paralysis

I did touch on this in "Part 1," but I'll add a little more detail. Sleep paralysis is a dream that involves the inability to move for a few minutes before drifting back to sleep. Biologically, this happens when the prefrontal cortex is active enough that the individual can open their eyes, see the room, and acknowledge where they are. It's different from lucid dreaming because the prefrontal cortex is not as awake as it is during sleep paralysis.

Is it possible for me to wake my prefrontal cortex to the point of sleep paralysis?

Theoretically, yes. If you were expecting a lucid dream and find yourself awake and unable to move, you'll be lucid enough to remember what your plan was, and the experience may be a lot more pleasant.

Most dreamers experiencing sleep paralysis aren't sure what is happening or how they got there, which can be quite frightening. Some sufferers claim to have had visions during the experience which made the experience much worse, while others say that it just made them uncomfortable.

As a frequent sufferer of sleep paralysis, I often experience visions and hallucinations during the event. Over time, I noticed that many of these hallucinations remained the same. For example, no matter what age I was or where I was sleeping, whenever I encountered sleep paralysis, the walls would wave and the pictures would melt.

This alone made it easier for me to deal with the experience.

Then, one night after I had become lucid, the most incredible thing happened; my finger moved.

Dream Figures

Dreams are codes from the unconscious mind. Before you can control and write in these codes, you have to know them. You can't speak Italian if you don't know the language. You can't communicate with a deaf person if you've never learned to sign.

I've constructed a small dictionary of what the various figures in your dreams might mean. It is important to remember that, regardless of the most common interpretation of these figures, what matters is what you know about yourself. Remember, darkness isn't always bad, and light isn't always good. Everything depends on what you believe. So, if your interpretation of your dream figures doesn't match what is mentioned here, you are still right.

- **Animals:** Seeing animals, predators, or herbivores in your dream is both intriguing and miraculous. Animals represent the deepest parts of ourselves, our souls, needs, and desires. The animal you see represents something you have forgotten about yourself. A fluffy rabbit symbolizes your more gentle and intuitive nature. Perhaps you've lost your compassion because of a furiously frustrating battle. If you see an eagle, it may be about your need for revenge, your hunger to hunt, and your need to point out the darkness in others. Remember, no animal is bad. They are complex beings simply trying to survive in the world. People are the same. So, watch out for these interesting creatures, and look inside yourself and find what you're missing.

- **Babies:** There is nothing like seeing a crying infant in a crib beside your bed in a room filled with gold lighting and flapping white curtains. Like seeing a fluffy white rabbit, the baby could represent your need to be vulnerable. The baby could also symbolize the memory of yourself as a baby, or your own need to produce offspring. It could represent a failed pregnancy - it might be farewell from the child you were never able to see. Look around the baby and see what else could help you understand your dream.

- **Being Chased:** When you're running from someone and sweat is dripping down your back, it's not always a good feeling. How you feel about being chased is very important. If you are anxiously trying to outrun your competitor, it could symbolize that you are running from something in your life. Perhaps you are running from a memory, a person, a secret, or a project. Maybe you feel overwhelmed and can't get away from it all. Dreams of this nature are a sign that you need to take control of your dream and real life, to slow down, and to stop the chase. You are not helpless. And if someone is making you feel that way, leave! You are strong enough, and you will find a new job, a new lover, and a new place to live. Just go. I promise you; things have a way of working out for the better. To be chased is not the only choice you have.

Alternatively, if you like being chased, it might symbolize you're entering a new and exciting career or romantic opportunity. There is nothing better than feeling wanted.

I remember one night in my early 30s when I finally decided to leave my job. It wasn't something I wanted to do. But, after months of coming home every day exhausted - emotionally and physically - from being treated badly, underpaid, and underappreciated, I couldn't take it anymore. I wrote my employer a letter of demands. At the time, I was responsible for more than half the company's clients and what I wanted was very little. I just wanted my salary to match the hours I worked, and lunch break at noon. I was paid for five hours' work, even though they had me working for eighteen. I wasn't even afforded a lunch break and had to eat quickly in between meetings with clients. This made me tired and uncomfortable because I was struggling with my weight at the time. I was sure they would accept my demands.

The night before meeting with my employer, I dreamt I was being chased - I did a reality check and remembered that I was going to hand in my demands in the morning and quit if they wouldn't honor them. So, I started smiling in my dream and skipping away from my chaser. It was a wonderful and thrilling experience. More people joined the chase. Each person threw flowers and pearls at me, which bounced off my pink aura shield and into the flowery fields surrounding me. I loved it.

I woke in the morning, went to work, and read my demands - my employer refused. I was crushed. Where was I going to find another job on such short notice? But, as fate would have it, within one week of applying, my experience at the company made me a perfect fit in more than ten alternative companies - all offering benefits and better pay. I couldn't believe my luck. My dream self was right; I had nothing to worry about.

If things aren't working out and you feel like you can't escape, that's a sign to perform a reality check.

- **Clothes:** What we wear or choose to wear in a dream shows who we are and how we feel about ourselves. If you often see yourself in brilliant clothing in your dreams, you might be an expressive, judgmental, and empowered person.

Alternatively, you may see yourself in beggar's clothing, in tattered rags and worn-out shoes. Maybe you are sad about your attire. If so, change it. Your feelings about your clothes might represent your need to change them. You might be harboring a lie that you are poor and unworthy. This is not true. You are empowered because you have scavenged and survived. You are business savvy and economical. You are strong and valuable, and if you truly wanted to change your clothes, you could. You are not helpless.

If you are happy in your rags, it might be because you already understand this.

- **Death:** Change is complicated and restorative, whether we are happy about it or not. Change is death, and death is change. If someone or something dies in your dream, it represents change. If you are falling off a cliff and suddenly black out, and you wake up in a sweat feeling as though you died in your dream; you did, long before the dream. You are changing, so much so that you refuse to let yourself fall off a cliff and die. You refuse to repeat the past happen or stay helpless. Change can be scary, which is why we feel our hearts racing a mile a minute when we wake up from such a dream. Change is scary, but not always bad.

As strange and dark as it may sound, there will be dreams of death that leave you feeling blissful. I have a confession - someone in my family is a convicted murderer.

It took some time, but my family did eventually disown them. The night they were sentenced to prison, I dreamt they died. I was so happy in the dream. When I woke up, I felt awful. How could I be happy about a loved one dying? How could I be so cruel to a person who had helped raise me? How dare I feel joy over their death in my dream?

Now I know that it wasn't their death that I was happy about. It was the justice that had me feeling so blissful. Look into your feelings and acknowledge them within the context of what is happening. You're not crazy, and you're not an awful person.

- **Falling:** Falling is a common occurrence in dreams. It symbolizes losing control. This isn't always a bad thing, yet most people feel anxious within these scenes, terrified of hitting the ground below. What we forget is that, in life, there are so many people around to catch us and who would go to the ends of the earth to save us. You need to keep reminding yourself about these heroic figures in your life. Then, in your dream, you'll be reminded that you are just dreaming because there will always be someone to help you when you fall.

- **Hands:** Becoming aware of your hands can help you become lucid, and their appearance and how they make you feel can highlight an important part of your psyche. If your hands are dirty or mutilated, it could be a sign that you feel guilty about something.

I remember going on holiday with my family and having an awful dream where my nails fell off. In the dream, I longed to wash my hands clean and glue my nails back on, but I couldn't do it. It was infuriating. When I woke up, I realized it had been weeks since I had cut my nails, shaved my legs, or applied moisturizer. It was during the holidays, so I had time to indulge in self-care, but I just wouldn't. I was so preoccupied with going away and being good to my family that I forgot about the most important person: myself. That day, I made sure to trim my nails, wash my hair, bathe, shave, and moisturize. I didn't have the dream again.

As disturbing as our dreams can seem, they reveal an important part of ourselves. In my case, my subconscious had sensed that I was slowly rotting away and needed to find time to care for myself and body. My mind knew what I needed, but I wasn't paying attention. Asleep, I was able to understand what neglecting myself was doing to me and my self-worth.

- **Killing:** You might find yourself facing an armed attacker. Killing, like death, represents a desire to change. That desire to change might be toward yourself or someone else.

When I was in my late twenties, I got involved with a man I thought was the "one." He was charming when we met but, over time, I bore the brunt of his severe anger issues. One night, I dreamt he was my attacker.

I held the knife and plunged it into his hands and arms repeatedly. It was awful and I hated every minute of the dream. What did it mean and how did it help me?

The following week, I packed my bags and moved back home. I left him because I was terrified that I would hurt him. It took me years before I realized the meaning of the dream. I hated his hands and how he would use them to hurt me, but I loved them because they were his and I loved him. Whether or not I would have killed him, I'll never know. But thankfully, my dream stopped me from ever having to live that reality. He's not in my life anymore, thanks to my subconscious opening up to me.

If you've ever dreamt of killing yourself or someone, ask your mind what it wants to kill, and react accordingly. Feel the guilt of the dream; feel the pain and the terror. Remember, your subconscious knows what these feelings will do for you, and it will be for the better.

Your mind always works for your best interest, so listen.

CHAPTER 11

Exploring the Psyche

Things to Try in Your Dreams

Flying

One of the most common activities in dreams is flying. Being able to fly is exciting, memorable, thrilling, and enchanting. It's compelling and reminds us that we are the barrier between the possible and impossible. Not even gravity is a limitation. Just look at the Wright brothers, the first people to construct an airplane, and Amelia Earhart, the first woman to fly across the Atlantic. Anything is possible, and our dream world reminds us of that.

I want you to fly through the clouds in your dreams and soar like an eagle over mountains and rivers. Fly wherever you have longed to go: Paris, Italy, or Africa. Explore the world as you have always wanted - no finances needed.

Meeting Heroes

Perhaps you'd like to meet your hero. Is there someone out there you've been dying to have a conversation with? An animal, person, or loved one? Now is your chance. Nothing can stop you, not even death. Fly through the world to meet them or conjure them where you are. Ask them the burning questions and get to know who they are in spirit. Shake their hand, or slap them out of your mind, for good. You can decide who they are in comparison to how the world has made them out to be.

Prepare for Interviews

But, if speaking to heroes and flying doesn't suit your fancy and you'd rather do something more meaningful, why not prepare for job interviews, speeches, or presentations?

Envision the room before you, conjure the interviewer, their personality, and their voice, then practice and say the words you'll say. Create different scenarios to help you navigate the paths the interview could take. By participating in a preliminary interview, you can get a better sense of whether this is something you want.

Use the time to prepare and understand things you could never know. Remember, no information is off-limits. And, if you really can't find the answers you want from within yourself, why not seek advice from an expert in your dream?

Revisit Your Memories

One dream experience I love involves revisiting my past and re-experiencing my memories. I like to re-explore who I was and why I made those decisions. Sometimes, when we look back when we're awake, we forget all the elements that led to our decisions.

A very wise friend once said to me, "No one knows the situation better than you at that moment it's unfolding." I loved it, and the words stuck with me. We were at a wedding, and I was asked to give a speech. I was so nervous about messing up my lines and the audience not laughing at my jokes, and my friend said this to me. It made me realize that our reasons for doing the things we do are because there is no other way.

There wasn't an opportunity for anyone to laugh at my jokes because, in the middle of my speech, the bride started to throw up. There was food and wine all over the floor. It was only an hour after everyone had settled back down that the groom informed us that the bride had cancer. No more jokes could be said that evening, and my speech was a segment of nothingness amidst the pain everyone felt that day.

There was nothing I could have done but stop talking and watch in horror as the event unfolded. Talking would have made it worse; it would have shown lack of empathy. I'm not an insensitive person and I do care. No words of wisdom could be given in that moment.

My point is, you need to explore your memories and remember why you made the decisions you made. You made them with plenty of reason. Don't feel guilty, and don't feel broken or sad about the past, because you did the best you could. This is how your life was meant to go. The reasons will become clearer the more you explore your past.

Conquer Your Fears

Another great experience is to conquer your fears in your dreams. Take a breath, open your heart, and jump off that cliff you've been afraid of. If you can conquer the fear that stopped you before, you're bound to feel that sense of pride and accomplishment you've been longing for. If spiders terrify you, try to understand them in your dreams. Befriend them and understand their existence.

For most of my life, I was afraid of heights. I remember one time during a school camp, we all had to go rappelling down the edge of a rock. It was not so high, but there were lots of loose edges anyone could have slipped from. I thought I'd be fine because I was looking up instead of at the ground. But at one point, I realized I was too far from the top and too far from the bottom. Stuck in the middle, I started to cry. There was no way to go back up, so I had keep going. I couldn't do it; I just hung there and sobbed.

Years later, with the knowledge of lucid dreaming, I went back to that moment to understand what happened and see if I could deal with my fear of heights. While looking through my dream, I realized that the ropes I was rappelling on stopped quite a distance from the ground. All the other kids were helped down by a co-coordinator, but in my dream images, there was no one. Someone had to come down to help me because there was no one at the bottom. I would have fallen through the air if I'd jumped.

I was just a kid. It's no wonder I was terrified to make that jump. I would have hurt myself. I made the right call in asking for help. A lot of other kids wouldn't have been able to risk their reputation and become badly injured. Now, I see myself differently. I look back on that moment in awe at how observant I was. My crying ensured that the other kids after me had someone to help them. The team was "on guard" afterwards - which they should have been to begin with. That sounds like one heck of a leader to me, not someone afraid of heights. Since this dream, I've been able to stand on the highest balcony and look down, unafraid of the fall.

There is no end to the benefits you can reap through lucid dreaming. There is no limit to the knowledge you can obtain. You can do and be anything you want, just as you can in your wake life.

Healing Yourself

Lucid dreaming can help you begin to heal yourself, your memories, your feelings, your body, and your heart. These parts of you have been damaged by all the lies society tells us. We lose and hurt ourselves until we are broken vessels.

You need to look beyond the figures you see in your dreams, manipulate the scenes, and find the hidden meanings. It is only in the state of unconsciousness that we can begin to believe in what we think is impossible.

You were told you're not smart, and as a result, you don't believe you can be successful - what they said was a lie. You won't believe this until your mind is open, which is the case when you're asleep. You need to open your mind up to these possibilities in your dreams. Take time to just observe what is happening around you, and when you have begun to understand your world a little better, start manipulating the events.

I remember one dream I had in my younger years. It was during a time in school when my two best friends would fight endlessly about anything and everything - from boys to toys, to gadgets, to cooking.

Consequently, I dreamt of a leopard and squirrel fighting. The leopard would growl at the squirrel and the squirrel would scratch at its eyes. It was horrifying to watch because I was afraid one would kill the other.

I was afraid that the fighting would change our friendship and destroy it to a point where we could no longer hang out.

I didn't want us to split as a group, but our relationship was becoming toxic. It was hurting everyone who was watching it happen.

"Stop that! Get away from each other. Either you will get along, or we can't do this! I love you both, but I won't stand by and let you rip our friendship apart. We've been friends for years; either we all need some space, or you two will learn to get along. Either is fine with me. I'll love both of you regardless." That's something along the lines of what I said - although I think it was more like "Stop it! Stop it! Stop it!"

Anyways, the animals in my dream stopped fighting, sat beside one another in a huff, and just watched me, never interacting with one another again. That's what happened in my wake life. I spoke to them, and they left each other alone, but they were still cordial. That was okay because they could still love and forgive one another. Sometimes, when two people fight too much, they cross a line that can't be uncrossed.

I was able to heal their relationship by healing it in my dream.

From heartbreak to soul cracks, past life curses, and yesterday's mistakes - there is no limit to healing yourself. You must find the courage to remember that you know how.

Taking Control

To be an expert lucid dreamer, you have to fully immerse yourself in the practice. Follow the guides and exercises in this book as often as you can, without depriving yourself of sleep. Read other books and become actively involved in lucid dreaming social media pages. The more involved you become, the deeper into your psyche you can go. Once you have become an experienced lucid dreamer, you can ask how you can take control of your life within your dream.

Ask what your future holds and, if you don't like the answer, ask your dream how you can change it. Ask what you need to do or who you need to become to get the promotion. Ask how you can afford to live in a beautiful house. Ask who you can become without a varsity degree - maybe it's a successful businessperson, a loving mother, or a community mobilizer. You have the potential to ask, so you can know and change the outcome. But it all starts with your dreams.

CHAPTER 12

Envisioning a New Life

In Ten Years

You can lucidly dream. What now?

Now, you can envision a new life for yourself, the one you always hoped for. Close your eyes and think about what kind of person you want to be in ten years. Where do you see yourself? What is your career? Do you have kids or a partner? Where in the world do you live? Do you have pets or friends? Are you close with your family? I want you to imagine what a day in your life will look like in ten years.

I was plagued with problems, sleeping on a mattress in my mother's home. I had nothing of my own. My dignity felt years behind me, never able to catch up. Time seemed frozen. There was either too much or not enough to do anything I wanted. I was pregnant, alone, unmarried, and scared. My mother was mad at me all the time. I felt as though I couldn't do anything right. I ate too much, and I couldn't hold a job. No one wanted a pregnant woman, a single mom, or a woman of color with so many problems in their office…

I closed my eyes and a scenario unfolded in my mind - my baby was lost and alone in an orphanage, wondering where his mother was and why she had left. I was a drunk mess on the couch. My mother had long abandoned me. Cats licked at my face.

I didn't want that for myself. My mind stopped, frozen on that last scene. It's as if my brain had glitched as it had gone off autopilot. A woman walked up to my sleeping form, shooed the cats away, and helped me sit up. Through my glassy drunken haze, I watched as she went back toward the living room door and took the hand of a little boy – my boy. She walked him back into the room and helped him onto my lap.

"Momma, thank you for the cakes," he whispered in my ear, leaning in for a hug.

"What?" I asked. The woman disappeared. I looked around the room. This wasn't my house.

An enormous Christmas tree sat beside a fireplace in a

beautiful vintage sitting room decorated in red and white colors.

"They were delicious, hun," said a voice next to me. My little boy sprang from my arms to hug the handsome man sitting beside us.

"Where did this all come from?"

My phone started ringing. I reached for it in my pocket to answer.

"Hi baby, I know I'm running late. I'll be there in a bit. You know how traffic is this time of year."

My mother's voice chimed through the line, happy and excited.

"Is that work?" the man next to me asked. "You promised that you wouldn't let the office call you in today."

As confused as I was, I ran with it.

"You're right," I whispered back. "But it's just my mom."

"Oh? Is she running late?" he asked.

"Yes, she's stuck in traffic."

"So, she finally took the car we got her and not the bus? Phew, that's so great. Looks like it will be a good Christmas. We might convince her to move to that beautiful house by the coast after all."

"Maybe," I said. He kissed my cheek and took our son into the kitchen.

"Is that Walton? You tell him I don't want to hear any more about that beach house," my mother added through the phone.

"Yes mom," I lied with a smile. "I'll see you soon."

It was just a dream, but it was enough to get me off the mattress and restart my life.

Every time I felt let down and helpless, I'd look back on that dream and delve a little deeper. I realized I didn't want the jobs I'd applied for. Why would I want to work for a company that couldn't support a single mother? So, I chose alternative career paths, mostly ones founded by female entrepreneurs and women of color who could understand who I was, what I'd been through, and what I could offer.

I stood my ground and had a beautiful child; and, after two years, I was able to move out of my mother's home and into a beautiful place with a sitting room decorated with vintage furnishings. Like in my dream, I painted my walls red and white, although they started out gray. Sadly, I never married a man named Walton, but I did meet my partner (whose name sounds similar).

I never would have done any of this if it wasn't for that dream of what my life could be.

Where do you see yourself in ten years?

Write It Down

Put this vision into words and write down as much detail as you can:

- What kind of person are you?

- What are your interests?

- What are your strengths and weaknesses?

- What is important to you?

- What are your hobbies?

- Who are your friends?

- Where do you live? What does it look like?

- What is your career? Do you enjoy it? Are you good at it? How good?

Write down your answers and keep them close to you always.

You should read them before you go to sleep at night. Then, close your eyes and imagine the world you foresee yourself in. Slowly allow those orbs of color to morph into the living room of your dreams. Place yourself in that living room and decorate it how you've always wanted. As you fall asleep, recognize that you are dreaming. Use the cues described in this book to help you become lucid. Once you are lucid, walk through your life ten years in the future. Notice things you like and don't like; and adjust your desires accordingly.

Ask and Interact

As you sleep, ask yourself how you can become the kind of person you want to be. Let your dream give you an answer and guide you. Then, when you wake up, follow the path your dream laid out. Work on becoming this person, until you begin to feel the new you mold into your old self. Then, work on the next desire.

Ask your dream how you can learn more about your interests. Maybe you want to be a wine connoisseur or a pilot. Ask your dream how you can start this journey and delve deeper until they become part of you.

Ask your dream how you can develop your strengths and work on your weaknesses. Accept these strengths and weaknesses as part of you.

Ask your dream how you can make the kind of friends you want, where you can meet them, and what you need to gain their trust. Ask your dreams if these are the people you want around you. You might be surprised by the answer.

When I was young, I always hoped I would have lots of rich friends who would look out for me. But as I grew and learned how to harness my dreams to their fullest potential, I realized I didn't want very many friends. I wanted a few friends who worked hard in life for what they wanted, and who loved their families more than anything. That's what I have now: a few friends and a beautiful family. Wealth was always a condition of friendship for me, and I wanted to rise above that. I wanted more wholesome reasons for my choices. I didn't want to go sailing because I could afford it. I wanted to go sailing to feel the wind in my hair and experience the freedom. I didn't want to be friends with someone because they had money; I wanted to be friends with them because we could carpool our kids from school and help them with homework and challenges.

Everyone is different. If you truly want money and to know people with money, that is perfectly fine. There is nothing wrong with being a rich lawyer in a fancy house with three hundred friends who come for house parties on weekends.

If your life ten years from now makes your heart soar, go for it. Don't let my dreams stop yours. Your dreams are as right as my own. Follow them bravely.

I hope to see you on your fancy balcony one day, holding a copy of my book.

Conclusion

The term "lucid" implies a sense of wakefulness while asleep. Biologically, when we are lucid, the prefrontal cortex is alive and firing signals, triggering thoughts, and manipulating hormones and organs.

Lucid dreaming is simply the act of recognizing that you are dreaming.

Scientists and psychologists have, over time, over-complicated the practice - and understandably so. Lucid dreaming is a complicated phenomenon that can help us understand so much about ourselves, our bodies, and the world.

Controlling your dreams and being able to pull yourself out of difficult scenarios and into beautiful and inspiring settings is a task that defies logic. It's a splendid and empowering ability. Many celebrities have expressed that much of their success lies in their ability to have lucid dreams. Thousands of mathematicians, premium writers, and excellent students have attributed part of their achievements to lucid dreaming.

In the famous words of Rudyard Kipling: "If you can keep your head when all about you is losing theirs... you'll achieve greater things than you can ever imagine" (Dinobeano, 2009, para. 3). This is exactly what lucid dreaming is all about.

I have told you richly inspired tales of lucid dreaming and its benefits. I have given numerous scientific accounts that relay the existence of lucid dreaming. If you can't trust Stephen King, Einstein, the guys who experimented on cats, or me - trust yourself. Delve deep into your mind and explore the exercises and suggestions I've made. Just try it, even just for a laugh.

You'll find that, by analyzing your dreams, you can take control of them. You can live the life you always wanted. You can do anything.

Before I go, I want you to remember one thing: No rule says you must know how to lucid dream. You won't miss out on anything if you don't. However, you may miss out on who you could be.

Thank You

"Happiness springs from doing good and helping others."
— Plato

Those who help others without any expectations in return experience more fulfillment, have higher levels of success, and live longer.

I want to create the opportunity for you to do this during this reading experience. For this, I have a very simple question... If it didn't cost you money, would you help someone you've never met before, even if you never got credit for it? If so, I want to ask for a favor on behalf of someone you do not know and likely never will. They are just like you and me, or perhaps how you were a few years ago...Less experienced, filled with the desire to help the world, seeking good information but not sure where to look...this is where you can help. The only way for us at

Dreamlifepress to accomplish our mission of helping people on their spiritual growth journey is to first, reach them. And most people do judge a book by its reviews. So, if you have found this book helpful, would you please take a quick moment right now to leave an honest review of the book? It will cost you nothing and less than 60 seconds. Your review will help a stranger find this book and benefit from it.

One more person finds peace and happiness…one more person may find their passion in life…one more person experience a transformation that otherwise would never have happened…To make that come true, all you have to do is to leave a review. If you're on audible, click on the three dots in the top right of your screen, rate and review. If you're reading on a e-reader or kindle, just scroll to the bottom of the book, then swipe up and it will ask for a review. If this doesn't work, you can go to the book page on amazon or wherever store you purchased this from and leave a review from that page.

PS - If you feel good about helping an unknown person, you are my kind of people. I'm excited to continue helping you in your spiritual growth journey.

PPS - A little life hack - if you introduce something valuable to someone, they naturally associate that value to you. If you think this book can benefit anyone you know, send this book their way and build goodwill. From the bottom of my heart, thank you.

Your biggest fan – **Layla**

References

Aco Staff. (2021, September 10). *How to cope with Post-Traumatic Stress Disorder in college.* Affordable Colleges Online. https://www.affordablecollegesonline.org/college-resource-center/college-student-ptsd

Banks, P.. (2020, December 22). 20 Tips on How To Use Lucid Dreaming and Become More Successful in Real Life. *Get Motivation.* https://www.getmotivation.com/motivationblog/2014/07/20-tips-on-how-to-use-lucid-dreaming-and-become-more-successful-in-real-life/

Blackmore, S. (n.d.). *What happens when we dream?* Science Focus. https://www.sciencefocus.com/the-human-body/what-happens-when-we-dream

Borelli, L. (2016, December 12). *How the human body wakes up in the morning: Circadian rhythms, clock genes in brain regions influence perception of time.* Medical Daily. https://www.medicaldaily.com/how-human-body-wakes-morning-circadian-rhythms-clock-genes-brain-regions-406344

Caceres, V. (2019, March 15). *Why you remember—or forget—your dreams.* Everyday Health. https://www.everydayhealth.com/news/why-you-remember-or-forget-your-dreams/

Carr, M. (2015, April 8). Confront your nightmares with lucid dreaming. *Psychology Today.* https://www.psychologytoday.com/us/blog/dream-factory/201504/confront-your-Nightmares-lucid-dreaming

Cherry, K. (2022, October 2). *The 4 stages of sleep.* Verywell Mind. https://www.verywellhealth.com/the-four-stages-of-sleep-2795920

Cohut, M. (2019, September 27). *The science behind lucid dreaming.* Medical News Today. https://www.medicalnewstoday.com/articles/326496

De Borde, C. (2019, September 20). *What is dream tending?* Let's Explore Dreams. https://letsexploredreams.com/what-is-dream-tending

Dinobeano. (2009, January 3). Rudyard Kipling: If… You'll be a man, my son!. *Din Merican.* https://dinmerican.wordpress.com/2008/01/03/rudyard-kipling-if/

Eveleth, R. (2013, February 7). How to sleep like Salvador Dali. *Smithsonian Magazine.* https://www.smithsonianmag.com/smart-news/how-to-sleep-like-salvador-dali-13214669

Ferraro, K. (2021, February 25). *This is what happens to your brain when you lucid dream.* Bustle. https://www.bustle.com/wellness/what-happens-to-your-brain-when-you-lucid-dream

4 stages of sleep. (2020, June 5). Interpreting Dreams. https://interpretdreaming.com/4-stages-of-sleep

Gordon, L. (2021, September 2). *What are lucid dreams and how does the brain become aware that it's dreaming?* ABC. https://www.abc.net.au/news/science/2021-09-03/lucid-dream-mild-technique-rem-sleep-psychology-brain-control/100410796

Hammond, C. (2021, May 17). *30 common dream symbols and their meanings.* World of Lucid Dreaming. https://www.world-of-lucid-dreaming.com/30-common-dream-symbols.html

History.com Editors. (2018, August 21). *Surrealism history.* HISTORY. https://www.history.com/topics/art-history/surrealism-history

How lucid dreams cure PTSD, phobias, nightmares and emotional trauma. (2018, July 5). Lucid Forever. https://www.lucidforever.com/lucid-dreams-cure-Nightmares-ptsd-phobias-trauma/

Hurd, R. (2014, May 15). *History of lucid dreaming: Ancient India to the enlightenment.* Dream Studies. https://dreamstudies.org/history-of-lucid-dreaming-ancient-india-to-the-enlightenment/

James, S. (2021a, August 8). *Lucid dreaming in Ancient Greece.* Lucid Dreams News. https://luciddreamsnews.com/intermediate/lucid-dreaming-in-ancient-greece

James, S. (2021b, September, 21). *Can video gaming help you in lucid dreaming?.* Lucid Dreams News. https://luciddreamsnews.com/advanced/can-video-gaming-help-you-in-lucid-dreaming

kzt5196. (2015, September 10). The science behind lucid dreaming. *PSU.* https://sites.psu.edu/siowfa15/2015/09/10/the-science-behind-lucid-dreaming/

Lucid Dream Society. (2021a, January 13). *51 things to do in a lucid dream: Dream ideas (2021).* https://www.luciddreamsociety.com/amazing-lucid-dream-ideas

Lucid Dream Society. (2021b, January 13). *10 Best Lucid Dreaming Tips for Beginners (2021).* https://www.luciddreamsociety.com/top-10-lucid-dreaming-hacks

Marusak, H. A. & Hehr, A. (2021). *How does your brain wake you from sleep?* The Conversation. https://theconversation.com/how-does-your-brain-wake-up-from-sleep-151146

Mathews, S. (2018, April 9). *Is this mistake giving you harrowing nightmares? Expert reveals how sleeping in a hot bedroom could see you being chased by zombies.* Mail Online.

https://www.dailymail.co.uk/health/article-5594657/Is-common-mistake-giving-harrowing-Nightmares.html

McKenna, P. (2009, January 14). *Talk yourself to sleep: Paul McKenna on how to harness your emotions, shed anxieties and get a good night's rest.* Mail Online. https://www.dailymail.co.uk/femail/article-1114645/Talk-sleep-Paul-McKenna-harness-emotions-shed-anxieties-good-nights-rest.html

Meah, A. (2017, April 25). *30 inspirational quotes on taking control of your life.* Awakening the Greatness Within. https://www.awakenthegreatnesswithin.com/30-inspirational-quotes-on-taking-control-of-your-life

Misirlisoy, E. (2019, September 6). *What happens in the brain when you're dreaming.* Elemental. https://elemental.medium.com/what-happens-in-the-brain-when-youre-dreaming-7c0687c38d3

Muse. (2020, May 3). *The science of dreams: What happens in the brain when you dream.* Choose Muse. https://choosemuse.com/blog/the-science-of-dreams-what-happens-in-the-brain-when-we-dream

Napp, B. (2009, October 25). *What happens in the brain during a lucid dream?* Ezine Articles. https://ezinearticles.com/?What-Happens-in-the-Brain-During-a-Lucid-Dream?&id=3151788

Nield, D. (2016 January 5). *Neuroscientists have figured out how your brain wakes you up.* Science Alert. https://www.sciencealert.com/neuroscientists-have-figured-how-your-brain-wakes-you-up

Nunez, K. (2020, August 10). *The benefits of progressive muscle relaxation and how to do it.* Healthline. https://www.healthline.com/health/progressive-muscle-relaxation

Nunez. K. (2019, June 17). *Lucid dreaming: Controlling the storyline of your dreams.* Healthline. https://www.healthline.com/health/what-is-lucid-dreaming

The phenomenon of lucid dreaming. (n.d.). AloDreams. https://alodreams.com/the-phenomenon-of-lucid-dreaming.html

Sandoiu, A. (2019, September 23). *Why do we forget our dreams? Study sheds light.* Medical News Today. https://www.medicalnewstoday.com/articles/326421

The stages of lucid dreaming from beginner to advanced. (n.d.). Be Lucid Now. https://www.belucidnow.com/stages-of-lucid-dreaming

Suni, E. (2022, August 29). *What happens when you sleep?* Sleep Foundation. https://www.sleepfoundation.org/how-sleep-works/what-happens-when-you-sleep

SVAdmin. (2021, October 14). What did Einstein dream about? *Esotericism of Life.* https://secretsoftheserpent.com/dream-interpretation/what-did-einstein-dream-about.html

Turner, R. (n.d.) *Mnemonic induction of lucid dreams (the mild technique).* World of Lucid Dreaming. https://www.world-of-lucid-dreaming.com/mnemonic-induction-of-lucid-dreams.html

Turner, R. (n.d.). *Famous lucid dreamers: 10 celebrities who lucid dream.* World of Lucid Dreaming. https://www.world-of-lucid-dreaming.com/famous-lucid-dreamers.html

2 different types of lucid dreams: Benefits and risks. (n.d.). AloDreams. https://alodreams.com/different-types-of-lucid-dreaming.html

Zugor, S. (2020, June 26). *The complete history of lucid dreaming explained step by step.* How To Lucid. https://howtolucid.com/lucid-dreaming-history/

Made in United States
North Haven, CT
14 May 2023

36563748R00112